£1.25

D0783748

CASSELL CARAVEL BOOKS

A CASSELL CARAVEL BOOK

MASTER BUILDERS
OF THE MIDDLE AGES

By the Editors of
HORIZON MAGAZINE

Author
DAVID JACOBS

Consultant
ROBERT BRANNER

Professor of Art and Archaeology
Columbia University

Cassell · London

FOREWORD

Today the great cathedrals of Europe stand as huge and imposing monuments—the pride of local citizens and the wonder of admiring tourists, who come from all over the world to see them. But to many viewers these massive churches are cold and impersonal structures. It is difficult for modern man —even with all his engineering and architectural know-how— to visualize the manner in which these medieval houses of worship came to be erected.

The author of the following narrative explains that the phenomenon of the great period of cathedral building was a crusade. Midway in the twelfth century a fever to build fine churches began to sweep across Europe. Carried away by the contagion, the bishops and monks and masons and humble workmen created the architectural style known as Gothic, which still is considered Christianity's greatest contribution to the world's art and architecture. The style evolved slowly and almost accidentally as medieval man combined ingenuity, inspiration, guesswork, and brawn to create a fitting monument to his faith in God; but once it had evolved, it matured quickly and spread across the Continent. The great cathedrals, then, are far more than a testimony to man's creative ability: they are hymns to his faith in a Divine Being.

Because the cathedral crusade was such an absorbing and abiding activity of the Middle Ages, it was memorialized in numerous manuscript illuminations, paintings, carvings, and statues. Together with photographs of the great cathedrals as they appear today, these historic illustrations form a colorful accompaniment to an interesting, inspirational tale.

THE EDITORS

Opposite, "God as the Architect of the Universe," a thirteenth-century illustration from a French illuminated manuscript. During the Middle Ages the chief designer of a building commonly was known as a mason, a term that connoted lower status than "architect." But the cathedral crusade elevated the profession to the higher rank it had enjoyed in ancient times.

RIGHT: *Scenes from March and April are depicted in these sections from a thirteenth-century calendar carved on the Cathedral of San Marco in Venice, Italy.*

OSVALDO BOHM

COVER: *In this detail from a fifteenth-century Flemish manuscript, masons and laborers pursue their perilous work atop the scaffolding of a building site.*

PERMISSION OF THE TRUSTEES OF THE BRITISH MUSEUM: MS. ADD. 35313 FOL 34 R

ENDSHEETS: *The north portals of Chartres Cathedral, one of the most imposing of medieval Europe's many Gothic cathedrals.*

SCALA

TITLE PAGE: *A pinwheel of masons, a geometric study in the famous sketchbook of the French architect Villard d'Honnecourt.*

BIBLIOTHEQUE NATIONALE, PARIS: MS. FR. 19093 FOL 19 V

BACK COVER: *This section of the stained glass windows at the Cathedral of Chartres shows the activities of some of the working people who contributed money and labor to the building effort.*

E. FIEVET, CHARTRES

CONTENTS

AVE MARIA

SVGERIVSAB

I
ABBOT SUGER'S GREAT CHURCH

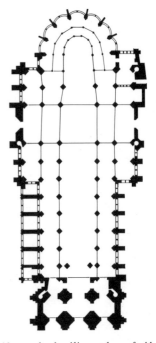

On an August evening in 1124 King Louis VI of France received word that his country was about to be invaded by the allied forces of the German emperor and the king of England. Surprised and unprepared for war, the monarch hurried from his castle in Paris to the Abbey of Saint-Denis, the old monastery named for the third-century bishop whom Louis regarded as, "after God, the singular protector of the realm." Kneeling before the relics of the saint, he prayed for the deliverance of France and pledged a generous donation to the monastery if he should return from battle victorious. Then he visited with his friend and advisor since boyhood, Abbot Suger of Saint-Denis, to discuss strategy before mobilizing his troops.

Above, the basilican plan of Abbot Suger's Saint-Denis church.

Although Abbot Suger understood that the enemies would be on French soil shortly, he was of the opinion that King Louis should not immediately take up arms. The two-pronged invasion, he reasoned, had caught the king's army off guard and too scattered to launch a counterattack sufficiently strong to repel the invaders. Under these circumstances, the monk continued, perhaps it would be better to call an assembly of all the most powerful churchmen and landowners in France and ask them to contribute money, material, and men to a united army of national defense.

King Louis had good cause to be skeptical of his friend's idea. Like so many kingdoms in twelfth-century Europe, his was little more than a loosely tied knot of political convenience. In an era when the line between Church and State

When Abbot Suger rebuilt the abbey church at Saint-Denis in the 1140's—and inadvertently created the first Gothic edifice—he had his image depicted at the feet of the Virgin on the stained glass window opposite.

was blurred, if drawn at all, the bishops, monks, and feudal lords of the realm were incessantly competing with the king and with one another for power. Louis knew perfectly well that at least half the men to whom Suger was suggesting he turn for help would be delighted to see him vanquished by the invading armies.

Abbot Suger, a shrewd politician as well as a scholarly monk, however, habitually kept a perceptive eye on the temper of the times. He detected a certain spirit in the land that he thought could, if properly stirred, work to Louis's advantage. In the Middle Ages all wars were called holy wars and all causes were said to be divinely inspired. Therefore, Suger proposed to interpret the purely political German-English invasion as an assault on the banner of Saint Denis himself. Moreover, he knew that few of those invited to attend the meeting could refuse—whatever their feelings about Louis. By turning the affair into a holy war, Suger automatically made it a matter of concern to Pope Calixtus II. As the bishops and lords of France were well aware, Calixtus, the former Guy of Burgundy and a Frenchman, would not take kindly to those who abandoned the cause of Saint Denis. They also knew that the pontiff was Louis's cousin and Abbot Suger's friend. To ignore an invitation from the king or the monk was possible; to risk offending the strong, stern pope would be foolhardy.

Abbot Suger's judgment proved correct on all counts. The influential men of France journeyed to the assembly at Saint-Denis, and once there, found the "holy cause" irresistible. King Louis led a large, united army to meet the invaders, who were already on French soil, but who had been counting on French disunity to work in their favor. When the foreigners saw the formidable forces assembled against them, they decided to forget the whole adventure. Without even giving battle, they turned around and went home.

Louis had not actually defeated the enemy, but he nevertheless considered himself the victor. True to his word, he donated a fortune to the Abbey of Saint-Denis, proclaimed it the religious capital of the kingdom, and guaranteed it a handsome annual subsidy. The already influential Abbot Suger became, after the king, the most powerful individual in France. So well did he serve the Crown that he retained his position even after the death of Louis VI in 1137. Indeed, when the new monarch, King Louis VII, went off to the Holy Land on the Second Crusade in 1147, Suger was named regent of France and was for more than two years the chief of state.

Saint Denis, the first Bishop of Paris and patron saint of France, was an early martyr to Christianity. Decapitated in the third century, he is traditionally depicted —as in the fourteenth-century figure above—after his execution, carrying his own severed head.

Although the Abbey of Saint-Denis was the most important religious shrine in the country, it hardly looked the part. Abbot Suger had had trouble enough keeping the monastery in reasonably good repair, but after the events of 1124, the frequent festivals and steady stream of pilgrims took their toll and threatened to destroy the church at the very moment of its glory. On several occasions people were trampled to death by mobs that were overanxious to pray before the relics of Saint Denis. Walls, pillars, and floors were cracking. The three-hundred-year-old abbey church simply was not large enough to accommodate the ever-increasing crowds; and as far as Abbot Suger was concerned, it was not grand enough either. The people, he felt, deserved something better. And he was determined that the new sanctuary be unlike any monument yet built in Christendom—a magnificent shrine to the glory of God and God's gift of life. But first of all, it would be for the people.

Suger's very genuine concern and affection for the common people were his noblest characteristics. The son of poor parents just a cut above the illiterate serfs of feudal Europe, he was born about 1082 not far from Saint-Denis. At the age of ten he entered the abbey for an education, and the abbot, named Adam, was impressed with his good nature and intelligence and made him the companion of the Dauphin, Louis (the future Louis VI), whose father had sent him to Abbot Adam for his schooling. The prince and Suger became friends for life.

Suger took his vows as a monk in 1106 and became Abbot Adam's most valuable assistant. Most frequently he was called upon to investigate and cure the financial troubles of districts under the control of Saint-Denis. (Many parts of Europe in the Middle Ages were governed under a system called mortmain, in which the Church was the legal owner of all property within its province and therefore could demand any percentage of anything made or grown in the area. Churchmen like Abbot Adam were fair in their demands, using mortmain as a reasonable taxation system; but many others were unreasonable, leaving the peasants only the most meager fruits of their labors.)

On his assignments Brother Suger discovered that when a formerly prosperous district suddenly reduced its contributions to Saint-Denis, it was, as often as not, because local Church officials were demanding too much from the people. Invariably ordering the obligations under mortmain reduced, the young monk also made a practice of involving the peasants in the affairs of the Church; drawing

In the above manuscript illustration, the Bishop of Paris dedicates the Fair of the Lendit, an annual fete held on the grounds of the Abbey of Saint-Denis.

people and religion closer together became a lifelong cause for him. In addition to his diplomatic, administrative, and scholarly skills, Suger once demonstrated a military flair, when, unarmed, he led a peasant army against the troops of a land baron who had been looting farms at night.

When Abbot Adam died in 1122, Pope Calixtus, with the enthusiastic approval of Suger's former companion Louis—then King Louis VI—appointed the enterprising forty-year-old monk abbot of Saint-Denis. A large dominion near Paris, Saint-Denis included more than one hundred towns, villages, and manors, and as many parish churches.

Now closely involved with all the affairs of state, Suger became Louis's ablest diplomat and wisest advisor. Thus it was natural for Louis to turn to Suger in 1124, when France was under siege. As always, his intelligence, common sense, and fairness were blended with his finest trait—his affection for people, be they kings, popes, farmers, or beggars. And it was for all of them that he wanted to build the most wonderful church ever constructed.

In 1125 Abbot Suger let the word go out that a new abbey church was to be built at Saint-Denis, and the response was testimony to the regard in which he was held. Gifts of goods and money arrived from bishops, lords, merchants, and craftsmen throughout the realm. Pilgrims with neither money nor material to give started the custom of harnessing themselves to carts and dragging huge pieces of stone fifteen miles from the quarries at Pontoise to the monastery, where they stacked them neatly for the day when construction would begin. With characteristic shrewdness, the abbot acknowledged the new prosperity of the abbey by suspending mortmain in the town of Saint-Denis. The gesture so moved the townspeople that in gratitude they took up a collection for the building fund. As the perceptive Suger no doubt had anticipated, their collection of two hundred *livres*—approximately sixty-five thousand dollars in modern money—represented a sum substantially greater than the normal intake from mortmain.

Year after year the Abbey of Saint-Denis prospered; the building fund grew; the stack of stone climbed higher. Except for necessary repairs and renovations, the monastery stood as it had been standing since the age of Charlemagne. Even the monk's constant duties at court could not explain away the delay. How much time would it take, observers wondered, for Abbot Suger to employ the masons, carvers, carpenters, and laborers required to begin? After all, it was not as though he had to build the church himself.

That, as it happened, was precisely the case: Abbot Suger wanted to build the most splendid church on earth, and he planned to supervise its construction every step of the way. He did not intend to rush into anything. In his mind's eye he saw it high, bright, light, majestic, warm, and inviting. He journeyed to Pontoise to select the smoothest stone with the most beautiful grains from the quarry there. When his carpenters told him that timber long and strong enough to meet his specifications was not available, he took distant, solitary walks in the woods, marked the tallest and finest trees, and on his return to Saint-Denis,

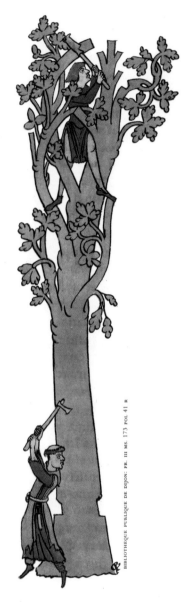

Like the monk in the miniature above, Abbot Suger found the tallest, finest trees to make lumber for his new church. The layman in the branches could represent a mason who claimed that trees so tall did not exist—and was about to learn dramatically that they did.

dispatched men to locate his markings and turn the trees into logs for beams. He made inquiries about the best craftsmen in Europe, whom he intended to employ to build his church. There would be no compromises.

He had the money, and he knew what he wanted, but still the work did not begin. It is said that he was reluctant to tear down any of the old structure because of a legend that Jesus himself had touched and thus sanctified the original walls. And beyond that, a philosophical uncertainty also restrained Abbot Suger.

Most influential churchmen of the era, including Suger's good friend Bernard of Clairvaux (Saint Bernard), were advocates of the simple, pious life. They preached that meditation, prayer, self-discipline, and personal sacrifice—not material things—provided all the comfort that the true believer needed. Following the brief life of sacrifice, they said, was an eternity of unimaginable loveliness—a more than fair exchange. Oddly enough, some of the least penitential clerics and nobles went along with this view, since it seemed to be effective when applied to the miserably bleak life of the medieval peasant. But the peasantry had few material things to corrupt it. Accordingly, while the churches of the early Middle Ages often were quite beautiful, they did tend to be dark, cold, and somber—as overbearing as the theology of the time.

Abbot Suger accepted the idea of self-discipline and personal sacrifice, but only up to a point. He had a natural affection for the elaborate over the plain, and he relished good food and drink. But despite the fact that the best of everything was available to him at the court, which he so frequently attended, he lived simply. His monastery cell was small and sparsely furnished, and he took the food and wine he loved in moderate portions. The point at which he drew the line, however, was just before seriousness turned to somberness. He absolutely refused to curb his major excesses—his affection for good company, good talk, and good laughter. After a long day at court or on a diplomatic mission, he as likely as not could be found long past midnight in the abbey dining hall, conversing with his monks, reciting Latin poetry for them, or telling them stories of pompous courtesans and hypocritical priests, his hearty laughter encouraging theirs.

The prevailing style of church architecture fell on the wrong side of Abbot Suger's line: the buildings themselves worked against his efforts to draw people and the Church closer together. A man of his perceptiveness, compassion,

Plated with gold and silver and richly bejeweled, the chalice pictured above was among Abbot Suger's most valued possessions. It reveals the influence of Byzantine styles on the ornamentation of West European arts.

and intelligence could not have failed to understand that the peasant's outward devotion to Christ and Church did not go very deep. Illiterate and subservient to his bishop or lord, the medieval serf accepted what he was told because it seldom occurred to him to question—indeed, he was told that doubt would result in an eternity of damnation. His apparent faith, then, probably was as much indicative of fear as it was of genuine belief.

No theological revolutionary, Abbot Suger nevertheless felt that the constant hurling of threats was unnecessary and unworthy of God. At some time in his life, the peasant ought to be given the opportunity to feel God and experience His glory—that was why Suger wanted to build a lighthearted church instead of a ponderous one. He wanted high, vaulted ceilings and beautifully carved altars, bright stained glass and bejeweled vestments, colorful pictures of the saints performing their miracles and lithe, lovely sculpture on tall, slender columns. Most of all, he wanted light— glorious, heavenly sunlight pouring through great, high windows, tinted by the stained glass, highlighting the burnished woods, illuminating the pictures, dancing on the jewels and between the stone folds of the statues' robes, warming the worshiper and brightening his bleak, pitiful life, if only for a moment.

Abbot Suger's great fondness for the effects of light and his eagerness to incorporate these effects in his church were less indicative of his personal taste than of the theology that he followed. As did a significant body of Church leaders in twelfth-century France, the abbot believed that of all visible substances, light was the closest in quality to the substance of God. He believed, as St. Augustine had said, that Christ was literally, not just poetically, the Divine Light.

According to the philosophy reflected by this belief, light was Godlike because it unified all things and provided illumination, through which all things could be comprehended. In other words, God, all-knowing and the Maker of the universe, was best understood and best emulated through knowledge of all that He had created. Objects, moreover, had value measurable through the quantity of light incorporated in them. Brass had greater value than

Abbot Suger was unashamedly boastful about the sumptuousness and value of the altar decoration at Saint-Denis. In the panel opposite, painted late in the fifteenth century, the bishop is celebrating the Mass of Saint Giles at the still impressively ornate altar crowned by the cross of Saint Eloi.

lead because it reflected more light; silver was brighter than brass and thus was worth more; gold was the most precious of known metals because it shone most brilliantly of all. Jewels were valued according to their brightness and translucency; woods, stones, and fabrics were measured according to their polish or shininess. Similarly, to build a church that let in the light was holier than to make a dark one, for more of God's substance was allowed to enter. To fill it with things that glowed and sparkled was to increase further the presence of God.

Abbot Suger's interpretation of the philosophic approach to building was an increasingly respected one but still somewhat ahead of its time. He knew that inclusion of so many valuable objects in his church might be condemned by more conservative theologians, such as Bernard, as being lavish and unsuitable for a house of God; therefore,

Compared with later Gothic architecture, the Abbey of Saint-Denis was modestly proportioned. Nevertheless, the unity of design and emphasis on light characterizing the style were first captured in Abbot Suger's church, at right.

he waited. But in 1137—twelve years after announcing that he would build a new abbey church at Saint-Denis—he rather suddenly began employing personnel and even sending distant artisans the travel expenses necessary to reach the monastery from many parts of Europe. By the end of the year, work on a new narthex—the porch before the main portal of the church—was under way.

The reason for Abbot Suger's decision finally to begin building is as vague as his reason for waiting. Many scholars speculate that the monk simply had reached a point in his life when he decided that it was more important to do what he wanted than to worry about his position in the Church and the State.

The events of 1137 would tend to support this speculation. Abbot Suger was fifty-five years old—a ripe old age in the Middle Ages, when the average life expectancy was about forty. Louis VI died, and Suger may have reacted as many men react on the occasion of the death of an old friend—by entering into a period of reflection and introspection. Although he was on good terms with Louis VII, he probably had doubts about his own future role in the affairs of the government. Most chiefs of state prefer to surround themselves with their own men. His life had been long and full, his accomplishments many, and he had little if anything to lose. Finally, he went ahead with his plans.

The monk's enthusiasm was contagious. No one could know that the new abbey church at Saint-Denis would mark the beginning of a new epoch in both building and religion. Yet the legion of noblemen and clergymen that turned out for the ceremonies marking the start of construction of the new choir on July 14, 1140, sensed that something new was in the air. Carrying stones to lay for the foundation, the king and his courtiers, archbishops and priests circled the site and walked through the trenches, singing the eighty-sixth Psalm.

> Among the gods there is none like unto thee, O Lord;
> neither are there any works like unto thy works.

Then the great men of the realm stepped back, and when the laborers moved in to place stone upon stone, King Louis VII removed his ring and flipped it into the mortar used to join the stones. The others followed suit, tossing gems and golden jewelry into the thick mixture, and everyone sang again. It was as though they all knew that something somehow more meaningful than a new building was about to be begun.

OVERLEAF: *Although the church and construction devices in this illuminated manuscript are Gothic, the picture actually refers to an event of the seventh century. The crowned figure, overseeing an early reconstruction of Saint-Denis, is Dagobert, King of the Franks. When the monarch was buried there in 639, he set a precedent, and Saint-Denis became the traditional burial place of French kings.*

BIBLIOTHEQUE NATIONALE: MS. FR. 2609 FOL 60 V

LA MADELEINE OF VÉZELAY

Most truly great works of art sum up the past and forecast the future: like a masterpiece of painting or sculpture, a building said to culminate one style generally contains also some elements of a coming style. Such a work is the Church of La Madeleine at Vézelay in France. Begun in 1104, the Romanesque edifice has mostly round arches supported by the characteristic cylindrical columns, as on the west portals (opposite page); buttresses project along the side wall. But the tower (opposite), added later in the century, has pointed arches, and the apse (right) has Gothic flying buttresses. The sculpture above of Christ and the Apostles, in the geometric and linear style of the period, adorns the spandrel of the narthex. The nave of La Madeleine is even more strik-

ingly an example of architecture in transition. Although the decorated arches crossing the nave are round, the more-difficult-to-see diagonal arches (notice the X formed by these arches between the larger arches in the photograph opposite) intersect, making what is thought to be the first cross-vault in Europe. The same photograph reveals the striking difference between lighting in Romanesque and Gothic architecture. Although the nave has a clearstory—the row of windows at the top of the church, a feature more Gothic than Romanesque —the apse in the background is built in the fully matured Gothic style, with its much higher windows, and is in consequence much brighter. Compared with the *Last Judgment* sculpture, the figures at right, carved around 1200, are more naturalistic and were carved with a greater understanding of human anatomy. While the piers of many narrow cylinders of the Gothic were not used in La Madeleine, the large, unadorned cylinders gradually were replaced by the clustered type pictured below, right.

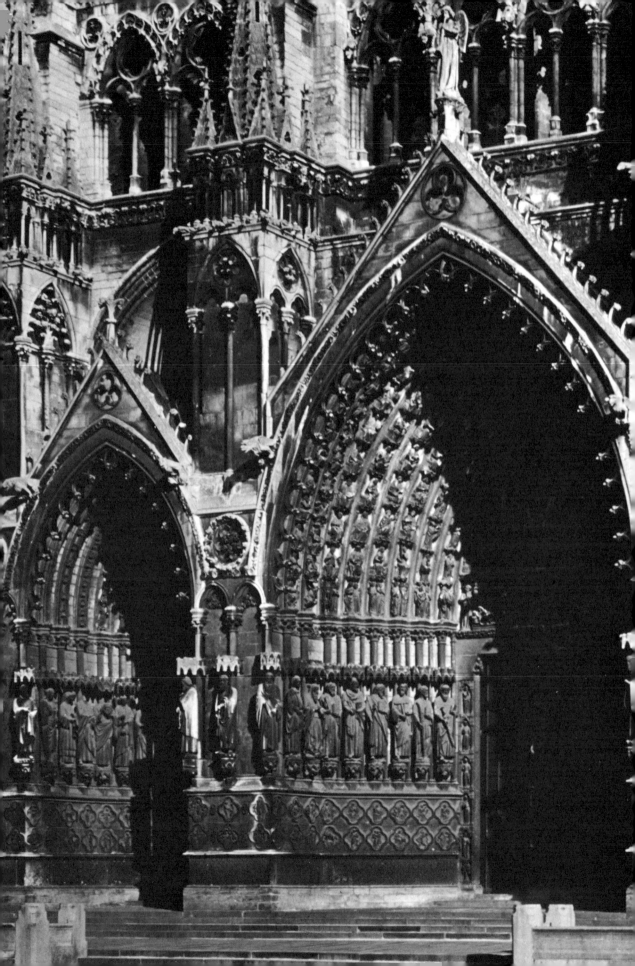

II

THE CATHEDRAL CRUSADE

The new church of the Abbey of Saint-Denis was the first Gothic building.

As did many artistic styles, the Gothic lent its name to an entire historical period. The people who made the style and lived through the period, however, did not call it that. It was named by people in a later age—the very people, in fact, who had resisted the style and who eventually managed to replace it.

Among the major nations of the Western Christian world, Italy alone was less than completely enthusiastic about the new architecture. Although they adopted some of its features and developed a modified version of the Gothic, the Italians by and large preferred to continue building in the earlier medieval style that came to be called Romanesque.

When the Renaissance flourished in fifteenth-century Italy, builders revived the Classical architectural forms characteristic of ancient Greece and Rome. As the Renaissance began spreading northward in the sixteenth century, Italian propagandists degraded the *forme ogivale* ("pointed style," as the Gothic was called in France at the time) by making it seem so much less civilized than Classical architecture. The artist and art historian Giorgio Vasari, for example, pointed out that while Classicism had been the product of two highly developed ancient civilizations, the prevailing western European style had been introduced by the Goths, one of the barbarian peoples who had overrun the Roman Empire in the fourth, fifth, and sixth centuries. Thus did the architecture of the late Middle Ages receive its permanent name. Until the nineteenth century pro-

Above, Jesus in Jerusalem, a carving on the Cathedral of Amiens.

Opposite, the west façade of the Cathedral of Notre Dame d'Amiens. As was traditional on Gothic churches, the tympanum (the area over the doorway between lintel and arch) was carved with scenes of the Last Judgment.

duced a revival of interest in medieval history, the world accepted this story as true.

Vasari's explanation had been almost wholly inaccurate. Gothic architecture was highly sophisticated and technically complex—much too complex to have been the product of a primitive mind—and of course, it had nothing to do with the Goths. It was, moreover, a genuinely international style, a blend of building techniques from all over the world. If anything, it broke free from the barbarian influences that had helped to create the Middle Ages and made possible the later break called the Renaissance.

The origins of the Gothic style can be traced back to the very beginning of the Middle Ages. In the year A.D. 326 the Roman Emperor Constantine I, who had made Christianity an official religion of his empire, moved his throne from Rome to the site of the ancient city of Byzantium, which he rebuilt and renamed Constantinople (now Istanbul, Turkey). From this base was established the Eastern Roman, or Byzantine, Empire, which quickly became the greatest and richest power on earth. Through a lively trade with the Middle and Far East, the Roman builders who

The first Roman emperor to embrace Christianity and to use the cross as his battle standard, Constantine is shown in the ninth-century manuscript panel above defeating a non-Christian rival outside Rome in A.D. 312. In 326 he moved his capital from Rome to Byzantium, which he renamed Constantinople, and there founded the Christian Roman, or Byzantine, Empire.

had accompanied Constantine were exposed to the arts and architecture of the Orient, which immediately began to influence the shapes of Byzantine churches. The style of building that developed is often said to represent a marriage of East and West. By the sixth century, that style had become fully matured and had produced what remains to this day one of the most splendid edifices in the world: Hagia Sophia in Constantinople.

Built according to a plan similar to that of the temples of India and embellished with rich, colorful ornamentation of Oriental influence, Hagia Sophia had large Roman arches and Classical columns; its huge central dome and smaller semidomes were neither Eastern nor Western, but uniquely, a bit of both. Almost as soon as it was completed, the basilica achieved an international reputation, and it was likened in its magnificence to Solomon's Temple in Jerusalem.

Meanwhile, virtually on the heels of Constantine's departure, barbarians from the north began streaming into Rome. They conquered, but the victors were so much impressed by the civilization that they had destroyed that they began to emulate the ways of the vanquished. Embracing Christianity with excessive enthusiasm, tribal leaders informed their subjects that they, too, were henceforth to consider themselves Christians. But the barbarians did not cease to be barbarians by virtue of a proclamation. Pagan rituals were continued, although now they were performed in the name of Christ. Eminently un-Christian methods— force, murder, threats, torture—were employed to make certain that the people lived obedient Christian lives. The period that resulted—approximately the sixth, seventh, and eighth centuries—is sometimes called the Dark Ages; for it was not the light of faith that turned Europe Christian, but barbarian force.

Barbarian artisans had traditions of their own. For centuries they had made richly ornamented armor and weapons, pottery and utensils, jewelry and roadside markers in a style that was intricate, linear, abstract. The infrequent church building that was done during the Dark Ages reflected the builders' backgrounds. Attempts were made to imitate the temples of the Classical world, with their seemingly simple, mathematical proportions and lifelike sculpture; but invariably the linear and decorative quality of barbarian art crept into the designs. The best art done during the period appeared in the illuminated manuscripts— handwritten and colorfully decorated books—made in the

HAGIA SOPHIA

Like the Parthenon to the Greeks and the Pantheon to the Romans, the church called Hagia Sophia—Divine Wisdom —was to the people of the Byzantine Empire both the symbol of and a monument to their civilization. It was a Christian civilization, and the church in Constantinople was the largest and grandest Christian edifice on earth. Originally erected in the fourth century by Emperor Constantine, founder of the Eastern Christian Empire, it was rebuilt a hundred years later by Theodosius II, who wanted the church to equal the ever-increasing grandeur of Constantinople. And a century after that, Justinian, whose Byzantine Empire was reaching its pinnacle as a world power, rebuilt the church again in approximately its present shape. The blend of Eastern and Western elements incorporated in the design is visible in the interior (left), where Roman-style arches are surrounded by Persianlike mosaics; and the layout (lower right) was the multidomed central plan favored in India. In many respects the grandeur of Hagia Sophia provided a model for the churches of the Gothic era—but a model to be improved upon, not to emulate—and it is doubtful whether many Gothic structures succeeded. In 1453, however, when Constantinople was captured by Moslems, the church was converted to an Islamic edifice, or mosque, and minarets (above, right) were added. Only then did the church called Hagia Sophia cease to be the grandest church in Christendom.

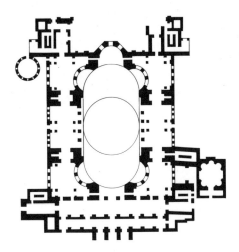

monasteries. Through these testaments the barbarian traditions stayed alive and continued to develop until a new and peculiarly Western Christian art was ready to emerge.

Charlemagne, crowned Holy Roman Emperor in 800, was anxious to establish a unique culture worthy of the western Europe that he had unified. Aware of the reputation of Hagia Sophia, he assembled artists and craftsmen familiar with Byzantine art in order to begin competing with the master builders to the east. Unfortunately, the unity Charlemagne had achieved broke down after his death, and few new or original buildings were erected during the next one hundred years. Despite the formation of individual and highly competitive nations, however, western Europe collectively became a major world power.

By the later part of the tenth century, the Holy Roman Empire's role in international trade was again almost equal

Much early Christian art in western Europe was basically barbarian art with Christian subject matter. The eighth-century bronze crucifixion plaque from Ireland at far left has the same linear quality visible on the fourth-century French spear mount at left. And the scalloped eagle above, made in sixth-century Spain by the Visigoths, is stylistically similar to the Lion of Saint Mark at right, from an eighth-century manuscript from Northumbria.

to that of Byzantium, and its potential military might was even greater. As its participation in commerce increased, the size and number of its towns increased also, and this stimulated an increase in church building.

About the year 1000 Western Christian builders began to develop a style that was part Classical Roman and part Byzantine—more the latter than the former—visibly influenced by the barbarian forms that had remained over the years, although these forms now were considerably refined. The empire's scholars, the monks, were understandably less than anxious to give credit to their Eastern brothers for the elevation of Western culture. Instead, they liked to stress—or invent—similarities between the ancient Roman Empire and the Holy Roman Empire. Accordingly, the style of architecture that resulted reminded men in later ages of Roman buildings, and it was called Romanesque, meaning "in the Roman manner." Calling it that did not make it that. The churches did have large Roman-style arches and Classical columns—as did the Byzantine—but otherwise the similarities were rather superficial.

The Romanesque style developed handsomely for two hundred years, assuming somewhat different forms in various countries. In Germany, for instance, the style became heavier and more angular, while in Italy, with its proximity to the Byzantine Empire, it grew lighter and more colorful. Then, as the eleventh century turned to the twelfth, the final ingredients with which the Gothic would be mixed were provided.

The Christian and Moslem worlds had lived side by side in the Middle East since the seventh century. If they

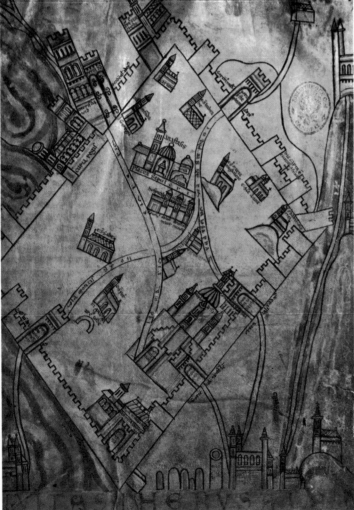

When the Crusaders marched through the Holy Land, they were enormously impressed with the Byzantine and Islamic architecture that they saw and began to regard their own church designs as primitive by comparison. At left, a map of Jerusalem made around 1150 reveals that the Europeans used the many churches in that walled city as landmarks. At right, a thirteenth-century German manuscript illumination shows two knights storming an unnamed edifice, doubtless to liberate it from control of the infidel.

had not been the friendliest of neighbors, at least they had
managed to maintain a reasonably peaceful coexistence. In
the eleventh century, however, both the long-civilized
Byzantines, the real descendants of the Greeks and Romans, and the Arabs were being supplanted as the principal
powers in their respective religions by more primitive and
warlike peoples. In 1071 the Seljuk Turks captured Jerusalem from the Arabs, wresting control of Islam once and for
all, and launched a series of invasions of the Byzantine Empire. In 1095 the knights of the Holy Roman Empire re-
solved to help their Christian brothers and to drive the
Moslems from the Holy Land. This led to the First Crusade.

Returning victorious to their homes at the turn of the
century, the crusaders brought to Europe new eyewitness

accounts of the glory of Hagia Sophia and an admiration for the graceful, uncommonly delicate and airy art of the Moslems. Perhaps the Moslems were infidels, but their architecture, it seemed, was more finely made than anything in Western Christendom. The lovely pointed arches and slender columns imparted a soaring, heaven-reaching effect to buildings of stone and mortar; and the craftsmanship was such that the visitor might forget that human hands had dirtied themselves putting it all together.

Perhaps more importantly, the crusaders brought home a new spirit. They had gone off to war crying "God wills it!" It became the cry of an era and gave the impression that all events—the most brutal war, the abuse of the peasantry, the laborious building of a church—were inevitable, divinely inspired, irreversible. All causes were crusades. The spirit needed time to take hold and grow and make its way into medieval thinking, but the First Crusade had given it the first push.

The spirit of the age was in many ways more basic a part of Gothic architecture than were the structural elements. It is often written, for example, that the style is characterized by a trio of structural units: the pointed arch, the ribbed vault, and the flying buttress. But one of the features, the flying buttress, was not used until 1178, at the Cathedral of Notre Dame in Paris. Yet it is Abbot Suger's church, which did not even have flying buttresses, that is credited with having been the first Gothic building. The reason for this is that structure is only a means to an end. The real qualities that make the Gothic style Gothic are light and unity of design.

Each church is supposed to represent Creation in miniature. Light, symbolizing divine light, illuminates the interior as though the walls were porous. All parts of the structure, including ornamentation, belong to the pattern of the whole—as though no part could exist on its own, as though the whole would collapse if any one part were removed. This is symbolic of the orderliness of God's universe and of the role assigned to all things in His scheme. Both luminosity and design unity appeared for the first time in the abbey church of Saint-Denis.

Between 1140 and 1144, while the choir of Abbot Suger's church was under construction, Bishop Geoffrey of

Early in the thirteenth century the cathedral crusade produced a succession of churches in the mature Gothic style, characterized by an emphasis on unified design and lighting—exemplified at right by Reims Cathedral.

Chartres found his frequent visits to the monastery particularly educational. His host and longtime friend was more than eager to point out the several design innovations at various stages of completion and to explain the building process and describe his experiments and discoveries. Geoffrey was especially attentive because his own sanctuary, the Cathedral of Chartres, had been badly damaged by fire in 1134. While reconstruction of some parts had been under way for several years, the work was not progressing so swiftly and so well as was the more ambitious work at Saint-Denis.

Surviving evidence suggests that Abbot Suger's principal interest was the lighting in the church. The fact that the church had the unified design that it had probably was a result of his concern with light and not something that the monk had planned from the start.

Unity of design, however, was what most impressed Bishop Geoffrey, particularly as it applied to the stone carving. The reliefs over the portals and the statues on the columns were extraordinarily graceful and expertly fashioned. Even more significant to Geoffrey, they seemed to belong to the over-all architectural design. All the sculpture fitted perfectly in place, looking no less important to the structure of the church than did the columns and beams. This unity of design, he thought, was entirely appropriate for a Christian church—especially for a great cathedral, which, in addition to being the seat of a religious district, or diocese, often functioned as an educational center and city hall. It was, he decided, just the effect he wanted for the new west façade that he was planning for Chartres, and he arranged to "borrow" the stonecutters from Abbot Suger. In exchange, he sent some of his laborers to the monastery to help tie up the loose ends and finish the church in time for the dedication on July 11, 1144.

The enthusiasm of those who had been present at the foundation-laying of Saint-Denis in 1140 was equaled by that of the guests at the dedication. King Louis VII was particularly pleased, and his approval—along with that of Bernard of Clairvaux—must have had much to do with the forthcoming success of the new style.

While Louis VII was leading his knights on the ill-fated Second Crusade in 1147–1149, Chartres West and the Cathedral of Sens were under construction. Along with Saint-Denis, these churches provided the luminosity and unity of design that were essential to the Gothic architecture of the future.

The Second Crusade further matured the crusading spirit. "God wills it!" now became the slogan for the bishops of France, who were suddenly aware that God wanted each of them to have a new cathedral. In fact, each bishop seemed certain that God willed that he should have a grander edifice than the bishop in the next town. Within a decade, cathedrals after the style of Saint-Denis, Sens, and Chartres West began to be built throughout northern France; by the century's end, the will of God had been revealed to churchmen everywhere in the country.

Early in the thirteenth century the contagion spread, and the great building boom burst the borders of France, going south to Spain and north through Germany and the Low Countries to Scandinavia. One after another the buildings rose, growing bigger, grander, and more elaborate over a period of four hundred years. It was a crusade that outlasted the Crusades, producing what was and remains Christianity's most extravagant and significant contribution to the world of art.

As for the abbot of Saint-Denis—his politician's sense of timing had been perfect, as always. No one can say whether or not Suger knew what would come of his church; it is conceivable that he did. He ruled the realm when Louis was off crusading, and then he retired to his sanctuary. At mid-century he might have been walking in the cloister or working in his garden as stragglers from the unsuccessful Holy War passed on their way home. He invited them to dine and rest, and of course, to inspect his new church. If they mentioned that they had been to Constantinople, he asked them whether his sanctuary compared favorably with Hagia Sophia—which he had never seen, but whose reputation had been an inspiration to him. Indeed it did, replied the knights, who were merely being chivalrous. The church at Saint-Denis had a lovely, peaceful quality; but at a small fraction of Hagia Sophia's size, it could not come close to the splendor and monumentality of the famous Byzantine edifice.

But if Hagia Sophia was a monument to an extraordinary age and culture, the Abbey of Saint-Denis was a monument to an exceptional man—one who sensed the coming of a new age. He died in 1155, before it flourished. His tomb was marked simply: "Here lies Abbot Suger." Nothing more elaborate than that was needed. He was buried in his church, and the church was his proper memorial.

The monks and bishops of the Holy Roman Empire, however, were very much concerned with matching and

In the illustration above, from a fourteenth-century Book of Hours, the King of France joins laymen and monks from the Abbey of Saint-Denis in a procession. Similar processions—without the monarch— often took place for fund-raising purposes. The reliquary on the bier is a model of the old monastery.

surpassing the splendor of Hagia Sophia. As the Byzantine Empire aged and weakened under constant pressure from its enemies, Western churchmen realized, with considerable pleasure, that they had become the leaders of Christendom. The Crusaders' "God wills it!" applied to their every act, virtuous or treacherous. God had willed that they should propagate the faith and defend it. God had willed that they should fight holy, and bloody, wars against the infidels. And God had willed that they should celebrate His glory by building the grandest churches on earth.

When the will of God was revealed to a particular abbot or bishop, the inspired cleric had to seek a papal bull— a formal declaration of approval from the pope—before going to work on his church. In twelfth- and thirteenth-century Europe, with the cathedral crusade under way, this was not at all difficult to obtain. After the bull arrived, two priests or brothers were charged with the task of fund raising.

Typically, the fund raisers would journey throughout the diocese carrying a bier bearing relics of the local patron saint. Addressing peasants and merchants alike, they recalled the exalted life of the saint and the many miracles that he had performed for them, and then they deplored the decaying condition of the church named for him. The speakers' eloquence and the sight of the holy relics usually moved the people, and they contributed money enough to get the building started. Frequently, however, both money and enthusiasm would dwindle, and the cleric in charge would have to try different methods to finance the work, such as reductions in taxes for contributors and special dispensations to the particularly generous.

Because populations responded differently from one town to the next, the length of time needed to build an edifice varied. The Cathedral of Notre Dame* in Paris was begun in 1163 and was completed about a century later. Started in 1195, the Cathedral of Bourges was abandoned, unfinished, in 1214; the bishop needed eleven years in which to raise funds adequate to continue. The structure was completed between 1225 and 1255. On the other hand, when the Cathedral of Chartres burned down in 1194, the people were so anxious to rebuild it that they contributed extravagantly and got the new cathedral finished by 1221.

*Almost all French cathedrals are properly named Notre Dame. Through common usage and because of its fame, the Cathedral of Notre Dame de Paris ("Our Lady of Paris") has come to be identified simply as "Notre Dame." The others are commonly called by the names of their towns.

Above, a hypothetical but typical medieval town, in which, characteristically, the cathedral is prominent. The illustration is a detail from a fifteenth-century painting by Robert Campin.

Ironically, one of the reasons for the success of the cathedral crusade—and the main reason that it was a cathedral and not a monastery crusade—was the rise of secular, or nonreligious, influences at this stage of the Middle Ages. As commerce increased and towns grew, the center of religious activity shifted from the monastery in the country to the cathedral in town.

Commerce also was responsible for an increase in the size and influence of the middle class—merchants at the upper end and craftsmen at the lower end. In the still closely interwoven affairs of Church and State, the best way for the middle class to achieve rank and privilege—not to mention salvation in an afterlife—was to maintain close connections with the bishop; thus were the merchants and craftsmen willing to donate money to the cathedral. Moreover, the prospering middle class was anxious to demonstrate its new high position, and one sure way to do so was to see to it that the cathedral in the town was bigger and finer than the one in the next town. The bishop, naturally, was only too willing to co-operate, and he, too, became very competitive: Longtime rivalries between dioceses now took the form of what amounted to cathedral-building contests.

Because of their growing financial dependency on persons outside the clergy and nobility, the bishops permitted the new cathedrals to be used for some secular purposes. In most towns, for example, each local guild—weavers, cobblers, metalsmiths, carpenters, and so forth—paid for one or more stained-glass windows. In exchange, the bishop allowed the cathedral to be used for guild meetings. Elsewhere, cathedrals were used for festivals, political assemblies, lectures, and as meeting places. Chapels became classrooms, and the nave (the main auditorium) was frequently a theater. The cathedrals became, in other words, civic centers. For the peasantry they were better homes than home, and the peasants spent as much time there as they could: something always was happening within.

The medieval serf may have been childlike and illiterate, superstitious, used and abused to the point of numbness; but he was not blind. As he began to spend more time at the cathedral, and as the breezes of secularism began to blow through the levels of society to his lowly position, his awareness of life's realities sharpened.

The serf knew that the feudal system under which he lived and to which he was bound was unjust, but he began to understand the causes as well as the effects of injustice. He began to perceive that his miserably deprived existence was not necessarily God's will simply because the priests said so. He began to resent not so much the contrast but the relationship between the lavishness of the Church and the poverty of his family. And very, very gradually, he began to realize that there was a point at which he could, and should, draw a line.

In the thirteenth century the people of Reims, France, drew such a line. In order to hasten the completion of his elaborate cathedral, the bishop of Reims imposed outlandishly high taxes and increased beyond reason the peasantry's obligations under mortmain. Reims was a great producer of linens, and by his own law, the bishop was entitled not only to tax the profits of the weavers' and linen merchants' commune, but to take a percentage of the value of all exported merchandise as well. The commune's tolerance of what amounted to a double tax on the same merchandise had been wearing thin for many years, particularly as the expenses of cathedral building led to higher tax rates. It reached the breaking point when the bishop, using the most fallible kind of logic, demanded still another tax.

The Reims commune, it seems, had agreed to send a substantial loan to a brother commune in the town of Auxerre, and the bishop insisted that the chest of money constituted an exportable item and therefore was taxable. Their tolerance exhausted, the weavers refused his demand for the usual percentage, and to further dramatize their opposition, withheld all their taxes until the withdrawal of the demand. But when, instead of withdrawing it, the bishop threatened to use force to collect the tax, the commune responded in kind.

Seizing the local military compound, the weavers killed the agent and took possession of the weapons; storming the cathedral construction site, they removed the stone and timber necessary to build barricades in the streets. Although it seems probable that the bishop did intend to call in the military, he abruptly backed down—perhaps he had received word that the local peasantry was likely to join the rebellion. In any case, the bishop diplomatically claimed a misunderstanding, withdrew his demand, and when work on the cathedral resumed, proceeded more slowly—and of course less expensively.

The bishop of Laon was not so diplomatic. When he refused to lighten his financial demands and his heavy-handed rule, the local burghers and serfs invaded the cathedral, burned much of it, and killed all the priests within, including the bishop. His successor wisely decided to work

46

The manuscript panels at left (probably intended to show events occurring simultaneously at different places on a building site) depict a revolt of the workers. Although the cleric in the bottom panel appears to be interested in the causes behind the insurrection, there is reason to suspect that the rebels are not quite ready to negotiate. The illustration at right refers to a feast of innocents, a periodic celebration in which the common folk masqueraded as such creatures as stags, hares, boars, nuns, monks, and bishops.

with the strong-willed peasants instead of antagonizing them. Establishing liberal government and maintaining a sympathetic ear to their complaints, he managed to harness their energy to the advantage of both Church and peasantry. He was one of the first bishops to make concessions for the secular use of the cathedral, and as a result, the new cathedral that he began in 1160 was built so quickly that it was usable after only twelve years.

Few cathedrals built later were operated with so many concessions to the lay populace as was that of Laon. Once a year, for instance, on the Feast of the Holy Innocents, religious services were conducted by choir boys; no clergymen were allowed to enter. While a boisterous satire of holy Mass was being sung, the rowdy townspeople laughed, threw rotten fruit and vegetables, and shouted bawdy remarks. But however irreverent this celebration, it was mild compared with the famous Feast of Fools.

People traveled long distances to Laon for this annual mockery of the ways of the rich and powerful. Presided over by a specially elected "pope"—usually the town idiot—it lasted all day. "Archbishops" and "bishops" and various "nobles" were elected from Laon's dunces, beggars, and pranksters: the more vicious their satire of nobility's behavior, the better it was received. After gorging themselves with food and drink, after singing and dancing and watching selected entertainers, the participants climaxed the day with the grand procession of the "Ragamuffins," which was in form patterned after the processions of the high

Among the more unusual sights on Gothic architecture anywhere are the oxen carved on the towers of Laon Cathedral, right. The animal figures were included at the insistence of the fiercely independent Laon farmers, who wanted to be symbolically represented on the church alongside the saints.

clergy. The most prominent places, however, were given to the dirtiest, sloppiest, and clumsiest marchers present.

Even the farmers and wine makers around Laon asserted their importance. They may not have had anything comparable to the Feast of Fools, but they wanted permanent evidence of their contributions on the cathedral itself. As a result, the bishop ordered statues of oxen to be placed on the roof and figures of grapevines to be carved clearly on the column capitals.

Few bishops were as vulnerable, and few had to be as attentive to the demands of the local citizenry, as was the bishop of Laon. His cathedral is, admittedly, an extreme example of the growth of secular influence on church building; nevertheless, religion was faltering as the primary force behind the development of architecture. The wish to demonstrate one's power, the desire for personal glory, the spirit of competitiveness, the craving for what we might call status symbols—these very human elements were to a significant extent responsible for the spread of the Gothic style.

Competition was particularly significant. As bishops

began insisting on bigger, taller, grander churches, masons had to develop new structural systems to make such size, weight, and height possible. Styles of sculpture advanced by leaps and bounds as one bishop insisted that the carving on his cathedral must be better than that on the church of a colleague. Characteristically, the bishop of Reims decided not to install his new grand portal when he saw that the portal of Amiens Cathedral was finer. In fact, he hired the sculptor Jean le Loup, who had done the portal at Amiens, and simply instructed him to outdo his own work. Jean, incidentally, did just that.

Bishops and monks soon lost control of the cathedral crusade. Building had become so complex, and it had changed so rapidly, that keeping up with the technical developments became a full-time job. Masons became architects in the modern sense. Like sculptors, they were concerned primarily with artistic principles and with demonstrating their technical skills. Some clergymen thought that they cared too much for virtuosity and not enough for spirituality. In time it came to be said that the religious figures on the church of La Sainte-Chapelle in Paris resembled the statuary at Reims but that they had lost their souls.

The incongruity of the oxen carvings on Laon Cathedral is captured in the exaggerated drawing at left, which is from the now-famous sketchbook of the medieval mason Villard d'Honnecourt.

49

III

BISHOPS AND BUILDERS

If the monks and bishops of France could have foreseen the effect of their building competition on the mason, they might have willingly abandoned the cathedral crusade at the outset. Years of association had taught them that the mason tended to be a stubborn, argumentative sort, secretive and given to complaining about lack of funds, inadequate materials, and conditions in general. But this had been no real problem for as long as the churchmen themselves had understood the fundamental principles of building. Their problem started when they allowed—indeed, encouraged—the international Gothic style to emerge, with all its technical complexity and changeability. Thus, they became dependent on the mason instead of the other way around, for only the mason had the time to study the building profession and the experience to adapt to the constant stylistic changes.

Above, a mason's compass appears in a medieval manuscript initial.

As soon as he realized how important he was becoming, the mason quickly asserted and flaunted his independence. He asked for higher pay, and he got it. He dressed garishly, favoring showy silks and satins and huge capes of bright solid colors, lined with gaily patterned prints. He let his hair grow long and cultivated an unruly beard—at a time when short-cropped hair and a clean-shaven face were signs of piety and self-sacrifice. His speech was peppered with curses; he was irreverent; he contradicted the bishop's orders for contradiction's sake.

The bishop was beside himself with anger but reluctant to respond too harshly. The cathedral crusade was, after all, a competition. To offend the mason was to risk having him quit and volunteer his services to a rival bishop for

Defying standards of monastic discipline, the mason of the late Middle Ages often wore a beard and let his hair grow long. The German sculptor Adam Krafft (1455–1508) depicted himself as a medieval mason (opposite).

The Flowering of the Middle Ages, THAMES AND HUDSON, LTD.

The drawing at right shows ninth-century King Offa, a contemporary of Charlemagne's, issuing explicit instructions to his master mason. Later, the matter of who gave instructions to whom was to be reversed, as the illustration on the opposite page makes clear.

BRITISH MUSEUM: COTTON NERO D. I. FOL. 23 V

whom he might build, for spite, a cathedral of matchless splendor. By the century's end, the Church, which still was powerful enough to control monarchs, was having a great deal of trouble handling the upstarts it virtually had owned not too long before.

In 1230 the Church decided that it had had enough. The bishops realized that they had allowed things to go so far because of their own competitiveness; thus divided, they had been powerless. Now they were determined to put aside their rivalries and unite. Only through a show of unity could they shake the masons of their worldly ways and force them to end their defiance of the Church. An order went out from every abbey and cathedral: The masons (for a start) were to shave off their beards and cut their hair short.

The masons refused. As they had done so often before with much less cause, they immediately called a strike; and all building in France stopped. That probably had been the Church's plan—to stop building until the order was obeyed. The bishops held firm. The masons held firm. The bishops made threats: imprisonment, trial for heresy, torture. The masons were unmoved. After a standoff of several weeks, the masons made an announcement: The order would not be obeyed. In fact, it must be rescinded. It it were not, the brotherhood of masons would systematically burn to the ground every last church, monastery, and cathedral in France.

Considering the enormous power of the Church, this was an incredible ultimatum. Nevertheless, the bishops backed down. Still long-haired and bearded, the masons gave the word to resume work, and the cathedral crusade continued. Thereafter, the Church rapidly lost influence over the development of architectural styles. The new relationship that was established between bishop and mason resembled the client-to-architect arrangement that has prevailed ever since. And the mason himself found his prestige, position, and prosperity rising higher still, until he was equal in stature to a university professor.

All that had been required for the mason to reach his fine new position was recognition of himself. Just a couple of centuries before his emancipation the mason scarcely knew that he existed, and in a way, he did not. Early in the Middle Ages, the only acknowledged professional masons were transients from Byzantium, fetched by European rulers to build in the West. These visitors taught the monks of the realm the principles of building. The monks were actually the masons, and they instructed local artisans, who were just a cut above the serf, in some of the fundamentals of construction. Little building was done anyway, and no precedents were set.

Just before the onset of the Romanesque era, some monasteries and nobles began maintaining a resident builder in a manner that did set a precedent—an unfortunate one. Uneducated and illiterate, this primeval mason was selected from the peasantry, not because he displayed talent but because of his strong back. If he was assigned to a nobleman, he had to follow his lord everywhere, and whenever so directed, he had to assemble the materials and personnel required to build whatever needed building— often an encampment or a temporary fortification. His circumstances were slightly better than those of the people whom he hired (or conscripted by the lord's order): they ate and slept in the barn if there was room, outdoors if not, while he ate and slept in the kitchen or sometimes in the servants' tents.

Even more unfortunate was the working brother assigned to a monastery. A virtual prisoner, he even was supervised by a warden, or foreman, whose job it was to keep all the laborers in line. Although his was the childlike faith of the peasantry and he was only vaguely aware of what the rituals of the abbey meant, the working brother was required to live according to the severe monastic law, with its deliberate poverty, long, silent sessions of study

Times were changing, according to this twelfth-century manuscript illustration depicting the building of the Abbey of Cluny. The mason, Gunzo, is talking, and the monk, Abbot Hugues, is listening.

and prayer, and periodic fasts. But whether he worked for a monk or for a nobleman, the early mason had very little to do with architecture. The actual plans were drawn by his master—most upper-class men were taught building principles—who gave them to the mason to execute. Essentially, the mason was a construction foreman.

Almost inadvertently, the mason became somewhat more sophisticated in the eleventh century—and therefore more valuable. As the rise of the Romanesque increased building activity, the mason spent as much time working on the construction site as he did waiting between jobs, which was a welcome change from the old days. He could not help but pick up a more than elementary understanding of mathematics, particularly geometry; and such knowledge improves one's ability to reason. Moreover, his master became more concerned with architectural beauty and sometimes sent the mason to distant places to study and sketch a new church or two about which travelers were talking. Travel broadened him: at times he even learned to read and write. In short, the mason was becoming a relatively sophisticated man.

The old system received its fatal blow with the growth of individual reputations. Romanesque architecture had stimulated concern with artistic beauty in architecture, and the First Crusade had revealed how backward western Europe had been in developing artistry in building. While the abbot or baron still was in charge, he began to appreciate that some masons had more sensitivity to beauty and more craftsmanly skill than had others. One such mason began to find himself "lent" (or rented) to gentlemen friends of his master. This talented mason was not blind. Finding himself working for nobles who had masons of their own, he started to comprehend that his work—and through it, he—was somehow special. So instructed throughout his life, a man may swallow the notion that he is of low birth. But shown that he is unique—that he can do what others cannot—he begins to find subservience intolerable and to crave recognition.

The bishops and monks contributed to the mason's craving, and to a certain extent, satisfied it. When, for example, Bishop Geoffrey asked Abbot Suger to lend him the services of a certain stone carver, the implication could not have been lost on the artisan: he was special. He began signing his name to his work, so that all future ages would know that he was responsible for it. More significantly, he began altering the style of work, adding an original touch

here, improving a certain technique there, anxious to make his mark for eternity as an original and inventive thinker.

Such beliefs were for the most part alien, or at least played down, during the Middle Ages. Medieval art was valued for its uniformity. And since faith guaranteed immortality, the medieval artist had, according to the prevailing morality, no business trying to achieve it through other means. Certainly men were proud of their work—but the work to be proudest of was work that most closely adhered to prevailing forms. Certainly art progressed from one style to another, but usually as a series of subtle refinements of accepted styles. Like every facet of medieval life, art was bound so closely to the Church and its dogma that a sudden change in style could have the same impact as a sudden change in theology. It was not a period that welcomed change. There was always the possibility that the overly spontaneous sculptor, having tried a brand-new approach to his statuary, might find himself imprisoned or tortured for blasphemy.

But the mason's new importance allowed him gradually

At a time when anonymity was the rule for most artists, the sculptor Gislebertus understood that both his talent and his work were unique. While carving the figures on the Cathedral of Autun in the twelfth century, he boldly asserted his individuality and carved "Gislebertus hoc fecit"—"Gislebertus made this"—on the stone tympanum above this avenging angel.

55

omine labia mea a
pctics. Et os meu anu

to go further in his departure from the rules, following the increase in the desire for physical liberation that took place in the eleventh century. Because of an increase in runaway serfs and insubordination, and because some masters were becoming more enlightened, masons sometimes were allowed to operate independently and for their own profit. At a few places they were permitted to organize openly; elsewhere they organized in secret. Wherever masons still were treated badly, neighboring guilds sent representatives to encourage disobedience. One very effective method was to withhold new discoveries. Having been sent a hundred miles away from home to study a new technique of mixing mortar, the mason would return to his master and claim to have been unable to learn it. Getting the buildings built became more important to the nobles than disciplining the mason, and still more masons were released from forced labor and re-employed as independent workingmen.

At the start of the twelfth century the mason was still a laborer, but he had his freedom and some informal organization. By modern standards his bargaining power was not much—he was still a pauper—but in the first half of the century he won a seemingly modest concession that proved to be his most valuable prize, tool, and weapon: his lodge.

The lodge was a long, one-storied structure with compartments for lunching, napping, dressing stones, and storing tools. One such structure, according to the agreement, was built on every construction site at the patron's expense. It was important to the mason for two reasons: first, it protected his possessions from theft and the effects of weather; and second, it provided him with a place of his own where he could be in comfortable, private fellowship with his colleagues.

Within the lodge the mason felt things he never had felt before, feelings that he lost when he left it: a sense of dignity, of pride in his trade, of importance. Not even his home and family, if he had them, could make him feel as good. By the time of the cathedral crusade, the lodge was beginning to shape the masons into a true brotherhood, with a unity unmatched by that of any guild. Most important of all, it

The subject of the picture opposite (from a fifteenth-century Flemish Book of Hours) is Biblical: the building of the Tower of Babel. But the setting, with the masons' lodge visible in the left background, and the material, such as the scaffolding and hand crane, are typically Gothic.

was giving the masons organization, and through organization, power.

By the middle of the thirteenth century, the mason's lodge had become a sort of school. Dining halls and dormitories, sitting rooms and studies had been added, as well as a library for the storing of architectural drawings. The Gothic had become as complex as any building system in history, and the masons had had to learn advanced mathematics and engineering. They had learned, as usual, from each other.

(Masonic lodges of modern times do not have among their membership an exceptionally high number of architects, and their involvement with the art of building is superficial at best. They are, in fact, men's social and sometimes philanthropic fraternal organizations, and they have no relationship to the masons' lodges of the Middle Ages.)

The most important part of a traveling mason's pause at a lodge was his description of the buildings that he had seen en route. Early in the Gothic period the hosts simply listened attentively and committed his details to memory. When the architecture became more complex in the early 1200's, the visitor drew the plans from memory, and the lodge masons traced the drawings over and over until they comprehended the principles. Finally, when the Gothic peak was reached in the second half of the thirteenth century, it became almost impossible to build except from drawn plans; thus, the masons began to keep their tracings and store them for reference. Before leaving, the visitor, of course, made diagrams of the building his hosts were working on, and he took them to other lodges. In this way each lodge came to have a library containing drawings of most of the important architecture under construction.

Later in the Middle Ages—especially in fourteenth-century Germany and Austria—the masons' lodges developed elaborate rituals and jealously guarded trade secrets, but it was not for the fun or romance of it that they did so; it was for their own protection.

In the Middle Ages two thirds of Europe's population lived in serfdom—almost literally as slaves of the land owned by their noble masters. By working a year and a day at some trade, such as masonry, a serf could earn his freedom. This was the path that many took. Having achieved his independence after so many centuries of deprivation in servitude, the mason of the Gothic era was as proud as he could be of his new position and prosperity. He attired himself in expensive finery and loved to travel first-class, stopping at the best inns, ordering the heartiest meals and most exquisite wines. Unfortunately, the mason could not long enjoy this kind of public luxury. Because he traveled so often—the successful mason frequently was employed on several projects at once—he had to carry enormous sums of money with which to pay for his enjoyment; and in his splendid apparel he was a riding invitation to the many highwaymen who welcomed his passage. As a result, the masonry brotherhood set up a system calculated to reduce losses without sacrificing wardrobe: the mason simply carried no money or valuables whatever. When the bandits were particularly brazen—as was often the case when local rulers were off fighting a war someplace—the mason might leave even his own horse and wagon behind. Whatever he needed was provided by his brother masons. It was seldom more than a day's journey between lodges, which became his inn, bank, and stable.

To prevent infiltration of the lodge by impostors anxious to steal building secrets and goods, the masons developed a specific ritual for the identification of visiting colleagues. Although the various elements of the ritual were elaborate and uniform throughout western Europe, they were apparently very well-kept secrets.

Arriving at the lodge, the traveling mason knocked on the front door three times, opened the door, called, "Do masons work here?" and closed the door and waited. The masons within removed their aprons, slipped into their jackets and hats, and left the workshop to receive the guest in the dining hall or sitting room. One of them—they usually took turns—picked up a chisel, symbol of welcome, and went to open the door. After an exchange of passwords and a secret handgrip, a prescribed conversation took place:

VISITOR: Greet the honorable mason.

HOST: God thank the honorable mason.

VISITOR: The honorable master [name of master mason at guest's home lodge], his warden, and the pious and honorable masons send greetings to you and your honor.

HOST: Thanks to your honorable master [name], to his warden, and to his pious and honorable masons.

The visitor then was admitted and given food, wine, and a bed for as long as he cared to stay. If he had come looking for work rather than merely stopping en route to an assignment, he was signed up if work was available. If not, he was directed to a site where jobs were said to be had. In any case, when the mason was ready to leave, his

OVERLEAF: *A royal inspection tour of a construction site is pictured in a fourteenth-century manuscript. The master mason appears to be describing the work of the stone fitter working on top of the wall. After being measured and cut by the masons outside the wall, the stone is lifted by the pulley device on top of the turret. An assistant holds the mortar, and the fitter puts the stone in place. On the rear turret, materials are lifted by a different device: a serf, climbing a ramp.*

BIBLIOTHEQUE STE. GENEVIEVE: PHOTO, GIRAUDON

hosts prepared provisions enough to get him to the next lodge, including a horse and wagon if necessary. On the occasions when he would have to stop at an inn, he also was given money. None of this was charity: the lodge required masons to travel in this manner.

That the brotherhood of masons was well organized and achieved strength through unity did not mean that there was no competition among masons. Indeed, the rivalries of the masons equaled the rivalries of the bishops in intensity and spirit. There was even an undeclared competition to determine which mason could display his name most prominently on his work. While most of them fared very well in this contest, the grand prize undoubtedly belongs to one of the masons—we do not know which was first—at Chartres, Reims, or Amiens cathedral.

These three edifices (and later many more) had gigantic mosaic spirals or labyrinths set into the floor, with the centers lying at the middle of the crossing. (The crossing is the section that is found between the altar and the main assembly area. It is, as a rule, the most bright, most airy, and most prominent part of a cathedral.) According to a precedent that was supposed to have been set at Solomon's Temple in Jerusalem, these precise centers were the spots to which all pilgrimages were made. At Chartres, having made his way on his knees across a tile labyrinth 768 feet long, the pilgrim reached his destination to find the signature of the master mason set squarely in the center. At Amiens and Reims the center of the twisting path reveals a bronze cross surrounded by likenesses of the bishops and the master masons who worked there.

The rivalries of the masons seem to have remained harmless enough on the whole—there was, after all, plenty of work to go around—but there were some unfortunate exceptions. The most tragic was Alexandre de Berneval, the late Gothic master and mason of Rouen Cathedral.

In 1439 Alexandre was commissioned to complete the crossing and to erect the two rose windows at the church of Saint Ouen, also in Rouen. The mason decided to allow one of his star pupils to fashion the northern window, while he went to work on the southern one. Apparently he finished first and went away, leaving his student to complete his work. Rose windows—large, round, ornamented windows that represent stylized roses—are quite difficult to make: essentially the artist must try to duplicate the delicacy of embroidery, but his material is stone. When Alexandre returned some time later, he found that his pupil

Above, a drawing of a labyrinth from the sketchbook of Villard d'Honnecourt; at left is the labyrinth on the floor of Chartres Cathedral as it appears today on the rare occasions when it is not covered with chairs. The medieval labyrinth represented a finishing line for pilgrimages. After traveling perhaps a hundred miles, pilgrims had to decipher the proper route to the center of the labyrinth before their sacred journey was officially culminated.

At the start of World War II the famous rose window of Rouen Cathedral (left) made by the jealous mason Alexandre de Berneval was dismantled to protect it from the oncoming Nazis. For some reason, it never has been reassembled, and boards still cover the hole.

not only had mastered the technique but also had created a much finer window than he had. Furious, the mason stabbed the young man to death.

Alexandre was hanged promptly for his crime, but Rouen, having lost its finest old mason and its most promising future mason, was heartsick. A monument to the two men was erected in the town—inanimate stone forever, master and student, murderer and murdered, glaring at one another unendingly, their dogs at their feet glaring, too. The figure of the youthful apprentice wore a rose—the rose, no doubt, of his inspiration and undoing.

As one of the outstanding master masons of the late French Gothic, and as an obviously insane killer as well, Alexandre de Berneval seems to have had the qualifications necessary to guarantee eternal fame. Yet through an accident of history, Alexandre is not nearly so well remembered as is a much less talented and much less violent mason about whose work much less is known: Villard d'Honnecourt.

Villard probably was born about 1200 in the tiny village of Honnecourt, south of Cambrai, and most likely was active in the second quarter of the thirteenth century. He may have had something to do with the construction of the cathedral of Cambrai, Reims, Chartres, or Laon; but it is very uncertain, and he was definitely not the chief mason at any. He is famous for one thing and one thing only: his sketchbook. It is the only evidence that he ever existed, and everything known about him has been deduced from his marginal notes.

Villard was not a very good draftsman: his drawings of churches were awkward and his structural diagrams were inaccurate. But he is an interesting personality in art history precisely because he was not especially out of the

In the painted sculpture at left, master mason Peter Parler is depicted bearing the Cathedral of Ulm on his back. The statue may be interpreted as meaning that the burdens as well as the glory of cathedral building were the architect's and that he could expect, at the very most, only the scantest help from royal patrons.

ordinary. Apart from his unusual decision to keep a sketch-book diary, he appears to have been a perfectly typical thirteenth-century mason. And his book offers the best look we can get into the typical mason's mind at this important stage of the Middle Ages.

Villard's sketchbook, for one thing, reveals how naïve the medieval mason still was in many respects. Many of his notations read like those of a child. Neither logic nor a sense of orderliness seems to have had the slightest influence on his organization of the parchment pages: on one page a bear, a swan, and an imagined city of God coexist. If the mason had intended to use the book only for his own impulsive purposes, its disorganization might have been understandable, but from his careful directions it is apparent that he intended that the book be passed along to the lodge as an instruction manual. "If you wish to make a good poppet [puppet] . . . ," he wrote, "copy this one."

Younger masons, no doubt, were helped immeasurably by Villard's hints. They must have been particularly grateful for the mason's most explicit instruction:

I want to describe how a lion is trained. The lion's trainer has two dogs. Whenever he wishes the lion to obey his command, and the lion growls, he beats his dogs. This puzzles the lion so much that, when he sees the dogs beaten, his own spirits are dampened, and he does what is ordered. If he is angry, there is no use trying, for he will do nothing with either good or bad treatment. Please note that this lion was drawn from life.

Villard's sketchbook also shows that medievalism was on the decline. The wide range of subject matter that he touched on reflects the broadening interests—mostly secular—and the growing curiosity of the artist. There are pictures of animals, insects, and machines—some of his own invention. (He designed a wooden or stone eagle for a church. Its special feature was a pivotal head that could be turned to face the altar during the reading of the Gospel. There is no record of whether or not the contraption was built.) He invented—on paper, in any case—a perpetual-motion machine. And of paramount importance, he made drawings of Classical Age sculpture from Rome and tried to draw the human figure within a circle or triangle or some other geometric framework, just as the ancient Greeks and Romans had done. It would be two hundred years before the Renaissance—the "rebirth" of Classicism—would take place; but the spirit was already beginning to stir, ever so faintly, and Villard felt it.

Villard d'Honnecourt, whose sketchbook tells us so much of what we know about the life of the medieval mason, had a range of interest as broad as that of many Renaissance men. Lion training was one such interest. Villard always took pains to mention that his drawings were made from live models.

THE DRAWINGS OF VILLARD

The sketchbook of Villard d'Honnecourt is like a window on the world of the thirteenth-century mason. It was an ever-broadening world, a world in transition, and Villard was a splendid representative—well traveled yet in many ways still naïve, interested in a wide range of subjects while in some respects remaining rather parochial. The drawings reproduced on these pages—all taken from the sketchbook—depict some of the things that attracted Villard's attention. Above, the crouching man is less an anatomical study than a rendering of the folds of fabric. Above, left, a page of architectural, animal, and human figures defined by various geometric shapes. At left, a bear and swan almost squeeze out a depiction of the City of Heaven. (Villard seems to have drawn wherever he found blank space, and the architectural rendering probably was the final entry on the page.) Opposite are the mason's somewhat oversimplified instructions for making a variety of devices: top, a self-operating saw and a crossbow that "never misses"; center, two engines for lifting; bottom, a carved, pivoted eagle that turns to face the deacon while the Gospels are being read.

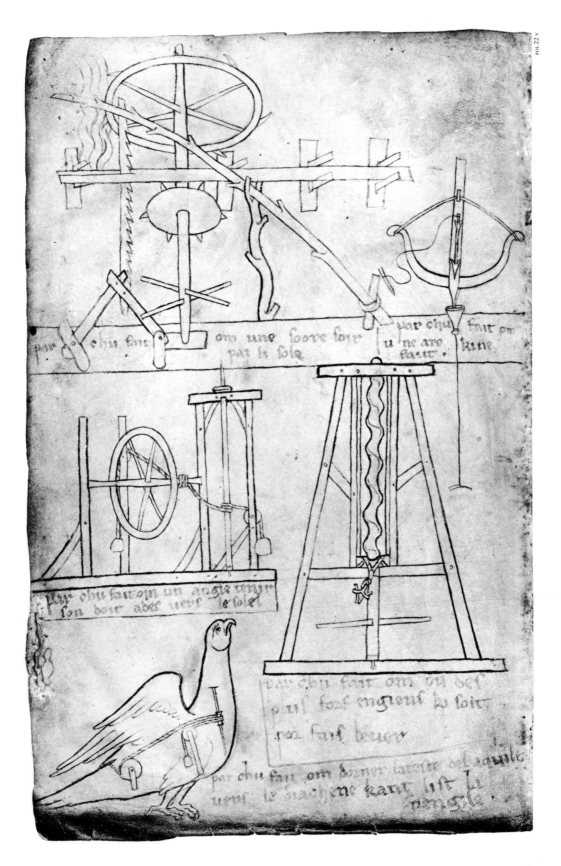

par ço chu fait . . . om une soore soie par li sole

par chu fait on u ne aro . kine fait .

Par chu fait om un angle venir son doit ader uevr le solel

par chu fait om en ser puil fost engient le soit por fait beuer

par chu fait om durner laroste del aquile uevr le siaghene kant list li temple

69

IV

A MASON'S LIFE

The sound of a mightily swung hammer striking stone was reveille for the legion of humanity waging the cathedral crusade. It echoed loud and sharp at sunup, rousing the workmen from heavy sleep and summoning them to their long day's work.

Within minutes—for unless it was summertime, they had slept clothed, and bathing was not part of their daily routine—they assembled outside the tent, dormitory, barn, or stable, or got down from or came out from under a wagon, or just stood up at the very spot where they had slept under the stars. Forming a silent procession, they faced east and followed the presiding monk as he led them in the singing of morning prayers. Then the orders of the day were distributed, and the men ate their modest breakfasts—perhaps bread and fruit—while walking to wherever they had been assigned. If it were the first forty or fifty years of the Gothic period, they would have to go about their duties in strictly enforced silence—a tradition lingering from the days when building crews were subject to the rigors of monastic discipline. To speak without permission was to invite a fine.

To some of the men the hammer's blows were like music. Among these men were the masons and aspiring masons and a few of the lesser laborers who simply enjoyed physical exercise and thrived on the strenuous work. Shaking off sleep and coming fully awake with the first loud clunk, they sang the loudest, arrived first on the building site, and set to work most quickly. The would-be masons stuck as closely as possible to the masons, eager to learn something each day that would take them a step or two

The stonesetters detailed here belong to a manuscript illustration picturing everyday medieval life.

The composite illustration opposite, from a French manuscript of 1448, illustrates almost every facet of building in the Middle Ages, as masons erect twelve churches (eight shown), one for each of the twelve apostles.

71

nearer to their goals. They knew that the masonic profession was one of the few in which they could enter as peasants and rise to a position of prestige and prosperity.

For many of the laborers, however, the signal began a day like any other day. Once, perhaps, they had entertained thoughts of becoming masons, but they did not have whatever it took. They were competent in what they did—hauling and fitting stone, laying timber, mixing mortar—but never rose to the level of craftsmen. Having fallen into the pattern of the construction man's life, they knew none other and went from one building site to another, looking for work throughout their lives. Also in this group were the men who did not care for the work but who did their best, grateful for the income.

To too many men the sound was a hateful reminder that elsewhere, at the same moment, the sun's rising was being celebrated by the more pleasant summons of the rooster, crowing farmers and their families to the fields. It reminded them of crops uncared for and rotting in their absence. It reminded them of overworked wives and children, who were alone in the violent world that was the Middle Ages. These were the peasant farmers who, along with many townspeople, had been conscripted by order of the Church to fill out the enormous labor force necessary to build a great cathedral.

To some people present on the site the signal was an annoyance: they turned over and went back to sleep until the sounds of construction made sleep impossible. These people were not the laborers but the uninvited guests who lived on the fringes of every camp where a church was being built. Some were peddlers; some were minstrels; and some were entertainers who could juggle, perform acrobatics, and do magic tricks; some were trainers of gymnastic dogs, singing birds, people-mocking monkeys, and dancing bears. There may have been times when the master mason sent for these performers to entertain the workers in the evenings and on rainy days when work was impossible and the runaway rate normally was highest. More often the entertainers traveled from one site to another on their own, living off the accumulated donations of the workers.

Groups of pilgrims and wandering friars arrived and departed unexpectedly from time to time. The pilgrims' arrival was welcomed by the masons. Journeying throughout the countryside in search of various sacred springs, rocks, and forests where miracles were supposed to have occurred, they were a harmless and eager lot, willing to

Inside the Cathedral of Gerona, panels of sculpture in relief depict medieval masons working at the building site. The earnestness with which they seem to be applying themselves to the work suggests that all of the figures are professional masons rather than conscripted laborers—unless they are simply putting on a display of diligence for the onlooking bishop in the panel below.

stop and help for a few days, expecting nothing more than meals and perhaps some old clothes for pay.

The arrival of the itinerant friar, however, was a mixed blessing. The laborers appreciated his being there in order to conduct certain prayers for their protection while work was going on, and it was handy to have a resident monk with the power to direct the elaborate rituals necessary to relieve afflictions and expel demons. But the workers learned that the unexpected departure of the monks often was accompanied by the equally sudden departure of many of their belongings, which had been left at the vacant campsite while they were at work.

The common laborer was the hardest-working member of the construction team, and he was the most poorly paid —if he was paid at all—but he was not entrusted with any responsibility that might require judgment. If he were assigned to the forest, he would be instructed specifically which trees to axe down. At the stone quarry he would be told which stone to cut loose: even then, he was permitted to cut only the largest blocks from the sloping quarry wall. The smaller blocks were chiseled by rough-masons—professional stonecutters who shaped the stone blocks for the outer structure of the church.

When the forest and quarry were connected to the building site by a river or stream, the laborers built barges on which to float the timber and large blocks of stone. First they would have to fasten hoisting tackle to the material and haul it to the barge. If all the transportation was overland, the material had to be hauled all the way to the site.

Although the men sometimes had oxen, steer, and horses to help them, just as frequently they themselves were forced to serve as beasts of burden. Smaller pieces of stone were transported by barrowmen. The one-wheeled barrow, requiring only one man to push it, was a luxury; more common was the wheelless barrow, carried by two men. The barrowmen were responsible also for the collecting and hauling of the rubble that was left in the quarry at the end of the day, for this waste often was used to fill in the space between the double-thickness walls.

In a Flemish illustration of 1482 (opposite), a priest visits a quarry where, miraculously, Nature appears to have provided preshaped stones for easy cutting, perhaps along dotted lines. The thirteenth-century drawing on this page shows carriers and a barrow man—men usually chosen from the ranks of the lesser laborers—working at their backbreaking assignments.

However hard the work, and whatever their attitude toward being there, the laborers seldom were victims of unchanging routine. The construction of a cathedral might be difficult, dangerous, at times even terrifying, but it was not dull. The master mason seemed to be everywhere at once, often accompanied by the bishop. When these two were together, an argument could break out at any moment, and the men were perfectly willing to suspend work to witness the exchange. Similarly, the master might find it necessary to reprimand one of his assistants, and his lecture was always a diversion for the workers. Equally entertaining were the fist fights that regularly erupted among the men.

Illness, injury, and death were commonplace but unwelcome reasons for work stoppage. Extremely superstitious, the peasants, who formed the largest part of the construction team, believed in sorcery, in omens, and in wearing enough charms to ward off uncountable troubles.

The Church itself went along with this primitivism and had its own rituals for the exorcism of demons, including unimaginably cruel tortures, conceived in barbaric minds and effected in the name of Christ. Because the Church constantly frightened the peasantry with grim portraits of the Last Judgment and pointed to floods, famines, plagues, and other disasters as examples of the results of man's sinfulness and God's wrath, the worker lived in perpetual fear. Most of all, he feared death without sacrament, in which there would be no chance for his soul to be saved. Sudden death was so close to him in the quarry and on the construction site that he insisted on giving himself every protection. The Church could not refuse without contradicting its own theology. Every misfortune on the building site was regarded as an indication of the presence of demons, and thus every misfortune signaled a pause in the work in order to deal with the evil spirit. Proper dealing required prayers to the appropriate saint.

If a worker had a fever, Sainte Geneviève of Paris was called upon to drive out the fever demon. Saint Blaise was in charge of sore throats; Saint Apollina looked after toothaches. A laborer who had been bitten by a rabid dog had

Medieval workmen enjoyed such stories as the one illustrated in the Spanish manuscript opposite. Top: a painter depicts a lovely Virgin and an ugly devil; the infuriated devil arrives. Center: the artist returns to work, but the devil destroys his scaffolding. Bottom: the painted Virgin holds the painter suspended, and the people give thanks for the miracle.

Medieval towns were frighteningly vulnerable to plague. When it struck, the townspeople wrapped their afflicted and buried them beside the church, to which they turned for comfort if not aid. Above the burial scene in the painting opposite, St. Sebastian intercedes with God for relief for the town while an angel confronts the plague's perpetrator, the devil. At right, a less ominous ailment is treated with some sort of potion applied with a stick. It is not known whether the patient's agony is caused by the earache or the cure.

a red-hot iron applied to the bite while the men prayed for help to Saint Hubert. Saint Sebastian and Saint Adrian helped to prevent plague and all the lesser illnesses that the easily panicked workers assumed to be plague. When one of the men had a nightmare, the next day's labor would be held up while Saint Amable of Riom was asked to keep the sleep-intruding demon away. Sometimes a series of accidents would upset the team so much that the fear of death would prevent work from continuing. Happily, there existed Saint Servatius, who was responsible for reducing the fear of death. The bishop for whom the cathedral was being built must have prayed most often to Saint Jude, patron saint of the hopeless cause—which was exactly what the construction of his edifice, with all these interruptions, began to resemble.

No work at all was done on the special days of Saint Denis, protector of France; Saint Thomas the apostle, patron of the mason's lodge; and whichever saint was the patron of the particular town. Feasts and grand processions were held, and splendid offerings were made in thanksgiving.

There was no saint more important than Christopher, patron of all travelers, protector against sudden death. He was revered especially by the painters, carpenters, metalsmiths, leatherworkers, weavers, and other craftsmen who remained on one site for a very limited time and then traveled to another. Unlike the masons, they had no lodges to eliminate the need for traveling with valuables and had to take their precious tools, gold blocks, skins, and fabrics with them on the roads. Although they traveled in caravans, they still were easy victims for bandits: the chance of sudden death on the highway was almost as great then as it is today. Even if bandits did not stop them, their wagons might overturn on the awful roads; and at night their encampments might be raided by packs of wolves.

Every major construction job employed various kinds and degrees of masons. The master mason was in charge, functioning much as does a modern architect. Under him were one clerk and several wardens. The clerk, or keeper of the works, handled most of the business details: he had to keep financial records and make estimates of the personnel and material needed, the time required for each building phase, and so forth. The wardens were the construction foremen, and often they were held responsible for errors made by the laborers, the attitude being that laborers should be assigned nothing beyond their capabilities.

Rough-masons cut and laid the stone. Freemasons shaped the soft stone used for doors, windows, and around joints. Cutters of hard stone were masons who worked in marble and alabaster, carving the statuary and decoration —they were, in other words, the sculptors. Most of the time, the stonecutters worked in the lodge or on the site, but occasionally, to save time and money, they would do all but the most detailed cutting at the quarry.

Masons usually were paid by the piece. Each stone that they cut was marked twice: once with their initials and once with a symbol corresponding to the spot at which the stone would be placed on the structure. Before the stone could be taken to the building site, the master mason or a foreman had to inspect the stone and mark it with his initial. If the stone later was found to be faulty, both the mason and the inspector were fined up to two days' pay. On the weekly payday the paymaster would inspect all the work done since the previous payday, record each mason's tally, add a bonus or subtract a small penalty according to quality, and compute the mason's wages.

The most serious mistake that a mason could make was to ruin a stone after it had been approved and during the actual construction. Since each stone had been cut to fit in a specific place, work could not continue until a replace-

Above, workmen complete construction of the scaffolding for what appears to be the tower of a building. This picture is a detail from a tapestry at Reims that was made at the famous looms of Arras, France, around 1450.

An arch in the San Marco Basilica, Venice, is carved with the sculpture above, showing workmen turning trees into lumber for the church. The naturalism that would characterize Renaissance art already is apparent in these fourteenth-century figures.

ment was fashioned. The mason responsible was fined and in some cases more extreme punishments were added. For example, there were times when all work stopped and the workmen formed a procession from the spot at which the stone had been ruined. The spoiled stone was placed on a bier and covered with a piece of black cloth. Dressed in the cloak of a mourner, the guilty mason had to walk behind the bier and sing all the chants for the dead as the stone was carried to the "charnel house"—a burial place. There, while the mourning mason continued with the necessary prayers, the stone was lowered into a grave. Then the procession returned to the lodge, where the culprit was beaten soundly by all his brother masons. Finally, when all the other workers were asleep, the fined, shamed, and bruised mason had to quarry a new piece of stone and hew it into shape. If it fitted properly the next day, all was forgiven and forgotten, and work continued as though it never had been interrupted.

Beneath the masons but above the common laborers in rank were the workers known as famuli. A famulus was usually a young boy who had been fortunate enough to attract the attention of a mason and who served as a mason's helper—dressing stone, mixing mortar, keeping the tools sharpened and in good repair. If the mason decided that the boy was capable of becoming a mason, the famulus served a seven-year apprenticeship, during which he was permitted to do some simple stone carving. The lodge and not the employer paid the famuli, thus the masons were very particular.

After his apprenticeship the youth was awarded the degree of bachelor, or companion. At this level he was assigned a work thesis to complete. If the foremen of the lodge judged that he had demonstrated his ability satisfactorily, the young mason was awarded the rank of master, which meant that he was a full-fledged mason. He celebrated his accomplishment by presenting each of the wardens with a gift of a pair of gloves and by paying for a feast for the whole lodge.

Although more and more young men were allowed to become masons as the demand increased during the Gothic Age, the shortage of masons never was eliminated. For one thing, the steady accumulation of stone dust in the lungs of masons made their life expectancy very short. For another, the well-paid masons began to realize the dangers and often worked only long enough to save some money to buy an inn or a brewery or a farm. Occasionally they would come out of retirement at the request—or insistence—of the bishop, but their fees were higher than ever, and they began to delegate responsibility to lesser laborers rather than take the normal health risks themselves. In consequence, the skill and pay of the common laborer began to increase. Like the masons before him, he was becoming uncommon.

The working day at the building site usually lasted until sundown, although sometimes the men labored by torchlight after dark. After a large dinner, some entertainment, and perhaps a game or two, the workers would return to the tent, dormitory, stable, barn, or wagon, or just lie down under the stars and go to sleep. They did not know it, but when they woke up the next morning, they would be more valuable to the evolution of their civilization than they had been the day before.

A glimpse of medieval building before the appearance of Gothic architecture is provided by the twelfth-century English manuscript at left. Since the series of arches beneath the roof would have been open, the construction worker on the ladder would seem to have lost his head over his work.

OVERLEAF: *The fifteenth-century French court painter Jean Fouquet dramatically depicted a typical medieval building site in the painting from which this detail was taken. Actually, the picture supposedly shows the construction of Solomon's Temple in Jerusalem, thus the saintlike figures on the building must represent Old Testament prophets. On a column to the right of center, Moses is visible, holding the tablets.*

BIBLIOTHEQUE NATIONALE: MS. FR. 247 FOL 163 R

V

THE PALACE OF THE VIRGIN

The "typical" medieval cathedral does not exist. Even though several structural elements are common to the Romanesque and Gothic styles of architecture, each great edifice is in some significant way unique.

This individuality among churches is one of the most remarkable characteristics of medieval building; for it existed at a time when rigidity typified attitudes, when uniformity was held up as a virtue, and when strict regulations prescribed procedures for doing almost everything. Clerics with typical motivations for wanting to build new cathedrals used uniform methods for raising funds, and they hired typical masons who hired typical crews to install scaffolding and construct roofing in typical ways. The German stonecutter used very much the same techniques as did the Spaniard, and both obeyed the same rigid conventions when carving statuary. Their representations of the Virgin Mary, for example, always had shoes, but God, Jesus, the apostles, and the angels invariably were shown barefooted. Each carved saint had specified apparel to wear, a prescribed expression on his face, virtually a predirected angle for the tilt of his halo. According to prevailing theological attitudes, only the heretic would dare depart from these standardizations. Aware of the severe punishments typically doled out to heretics, the typical mason stuck to the regulations.

Still, despite all the standards, there were no standard forms for cathedrals, no defined heights, widths, depths, colors—no typical cathedrals. Early in the Middle Ages, too little building was going on to merit regulations; later, the Romanesque and Gothic styles developed and changed

The Annunciation, *carved on the exterior of Chartres Cathedral.*

Opposite: from a distance, the Cathedral of Our Lady of Chartres looks isolated. Actually, the edifice is situated within the town of Chartres; only narrow roads and a plaza separate it from clusters of buildings.

so rapidly that there was no time to formulate standards. Building outdistanced theology.

Nevertheless, the Cathedral of Our Lady of Chartres is a nearly perfect example of a medieval church. It is important to keep in mind, though, that Chartres merely shows that the prevailing forces of the age converged to create a great building and to keep it alive and that it is not, stylistically, a typical medieval cathedral.

The main reason why the Cathedral of Chartres is so valuable to the student of architecture is that it is a product of the whole first half of the Christian epoch. In century after century it was built, destroyed, and restored or rebuilt. As often as not, as it entered each new phase of its existence, it retained something of its old form. Its evolution, then, paralleled the evolution not only of architecture, but also of Christianity itself.

According to Christian lore, the church of Our Lady of Chartres originally was built a century or more before the birth of the Virgin Mary. That it was a Christian church even before there was a Christian religion certainly seems unlikely; yet, like many legends, this one does have some basis in fact. For one thing, Julius Caesar in his *Commentaries* told a story about a place of worship at Chartres that had been built, he said, by the Druids. Modern archaeologists, moreover, have testified that certain portions of the foundation of the Cathedral of Chartres probably predate the Christian era. In view of this evidence, we could assume that the old church had been some sort of pagan temple.

The legend conceivably could be even closer to truth than that. In the first and second centuries B.C., Hebrew communities settled in lands throughout what was then the Roman Empire. At that time the Jews were very much concerned with the expected arrival of their Messiah and the onset of a glorious messianic era: in fact, false messiahs were quite commonplace. Although there is only sketchy evidence to support the supposition, a Jewish congregation in the town of Chartres, responding to the Old Testament prophecy, "A virgin shall conceive and bear a son," might have built a synagogue dedicated to the imminent appearance of the Messiah or to the honor of his mother. In any case, whatever the reason for its origin, the church at Chartres, probably resembling a Roman temple, was certainly one of Christendom's earliest monuments.

The advent of Christianity alone did not make the edifice at Chartres the very special religious shrine that it eventually would become. Changing times and the evolution of Christian attitudes over many centuries would make it so.

As Christianity spread throughout Western Europe, the barbarian peoples on whom it was imposed were inclined to look for and to cling to similarities between their new and old religions. Understandably, the earliest Christian heroes were warrior saints and martyrs who resembled pagan gods in a way that Mary, or for that matter, Jesus did not. The small minority of Christians who did form the cult that worshiped the Virgin probably had venerated a goddess before. Given to undertaking long pilgrimages and to making great personal sacrifices on her behalf, the members of this extremely pious cult treasured the church at Chartres and journeyed there often. As their numbers increased, their trips became frequent enough to make Chartres a major trade crossroad of France. So devoted were they that when the Aquitanian warrior Hunald burned the town and the church in the year 743, the cult of the Virgin led the townspeople to rebuild the sanctuary first and the town second. In so doing, they set a precedent that would be followed for many centuries.

Meanwhile, for administrative reasons, the Pope had divided his realm into districts. Each district, or diocese, was headed by a bishop. The bishop's home church, which was the administrative headquarters of the diocese, was called a cathedral (from the Latin *cathedra*, or "chair of the bishop"). Chartres was a logical choice for the location of a cathedral because it was a continental crossroad and a prosperous trade center.

In 858 the Viking leader Hasting and his troops attacked Chartres and set the town afire. When Bishop Frotbold and his followers retreated into the cathedral, Hasting followed, murdered the bishop, and put the edifice to the torch. Again the restoration—church first, town second— was prompt, though risky, for the natives still were harassed by the Northmen who continued to roam the country.

In this same century the cult of the Virgin, which had been growing steadily for several decades, was bolstered by the appearance of a relic that would further establish the position of Chartres as a sacred center of Christendom.

Early in the ninth century two representatives from the court of Charlemagne—possibly on a diplomatic mission, perhaps only to buy goods—went to Constantinople. During their visit to the eastern capital, they stayed in a lodginghouse run by a woman who claimed descent from a lady companion of the Virgin Mary's during the Holy Mother's

During the twelfth and thirteenth centuries, no less than eight Nativity scenes were carved in relief at the Cathedral of Chartres. The frieze above can be identified as one of the later works by its naturalism (evident in the soft-looking folds of the stone robes), which came to prevail in sculpture as art and history entered the twilight of the Middle Ages.

last years. To substantiate her claim, the woman in Constantinople produced a red tunic, which she said was the garment worn by the Virgin at the time of her death. Although the travelers probably were skeptical of their hostess' tale, it evidently intrigued them as they journeyed on to Rome, and there they did some investigating. Apparently, there was some evidence to support the old woman's story: according to available records, the Virgin had had such a companion, who did inherit a red tunic, and who did take it to Constantinople.

The pair of travelers decided that the sacred tunic belonged in the realm of Charlemagne, and they craftily planned to acquire it. First they sought a Roman weaver talented enough to simulate the appearance of a garment nearly a thousand years old. Then they searched their own memories, trying to recall precisely the color, size, and texture of the relic. Finally, under their close supervision, the weaver duplicated the fabric, and the two men excitedly returned with it to Constantinople, where they again took up lodging with the old woman. Whether or not the woman ever discovered that the men had swapped the old and new tunics is not known; but in any case, the travelers went back to Rome with the antique and at an appropriate moment had it presented to the Emperor Charlemagne. When Charlemagne returned with it to France, the prize had a powerful influence on the people, who were very much impressed with any tangible evidence of the Bible stories that they were told.

The sacred relic passed from Charlemagne to his grandson Charles the Bald, who made frequent pilgrimages to Chartres and helped to stimulate the growing veneration of the Virgin Mary. In 876 he presented the tunic as a permanent gift to the cathedral. About thirty-five years later it was stolen by invading Normans; this so angered the usually dissident or apathetic French lords that they united their armies under the command of Bishop Gosselin of Chartres. The battle was furious, but the French were victorious and the garment was recaptured. After that a goldsmith named Teudon was commissioned to fashion an exquisite case of gold and cedar to protect the sacred tunic.

The existence of the relic at Chartres, its apparent indestructibility, and the adventures surrounding its history were richly embellished and widely broadcast by troubadours. Throughout Western Europe, Christians began to interpret all this to mean that the Virgin did in fact regard the cathedral at Chartres as her own special palace. The

cult of the Virgin grew ever larger, and the Cathedral of
Our Lady of Chartres became, by the start of the eleventh
century, the best known and most often visited church in
the entire Western Christian world.

Inadequate to accommodate the legions of visitors to
the shrine, the old Cathedral of Chartres was rebuilt by
Bishop Fulbert in what could be considered the first stage
of its eventual form. Fulbert probably completed his
church, in an early Romanesque style, not long before his
death in 1028. In 1030, however, the upper portion was
destroyed by fire. Acting in prompt accord with precedent,
his successor, Bishop Thierry, immediately replaced the
damaged portions. By this time, the cathedral had assumed
the basic elements of its basilican plan, although it had no
protruding transepts and lacked the vaulted roof characteristic of the mature Romanesque style.

As we have seen, the fire of 1134 destroyed much of the
west façade of Chartres Cathedral, and it was replaced in
the Gothic style by Bishop Geoffrey in the 1140's. Throughout the twelfth century constant modifications and improve-
ments, the generosity of wealthy merchants, and above all,
the loving labor of townspeople and pilgrims kept the cathedral handsome and prosperous and only the slightest bit
old-fashioned. Indeed, the well-worn quality of the edifice
was cherished: here was one cathedral whose history, so
carefully recorded and so frequently remembered, made
the competitive spirit of the cathedral crusade seem rather
vulgar; here was one cathedral that needed no rebuilding
for rebuilding's sake. Let bishops elsewhere conscript hun-
dreds and spend fortunes—neither size nor newness nor
lavishness could match the traditions that made Our Lady
of Chartres the most precious palace in all of Christendom.

These traditions had made the town of Chartres a center of learning as well as a center of religion and trade.
Bishop Geoffrey had been instrumental in making the cathedral school of Chartres—long a theological college of
some repute—a magnet for leading Church intellectuals.
Saint Bernard, for instance, had been a faculty member
there during his most active and influential years. Nevertheless, the diocese was not perfect; it still was weak in the
face of attack, and its administrative operations were cum-
bersome, inefficient, and in places corrupt. But such situa-
tions were quite ordinary during the Middle Ages. The
affairs of Church and State were controlled by a complex
bureaucracy, and more than a few self-seekers managed to
work their way into most of its elaborate levels. Yet, com-

*In this manuscript illustration,
"The Miracle of the Virgin,"
townspeople and monks join forces and try to douse the fire en-
veloping a Church of Our Lady.
Although the firefighters' energies
appear to be failing, the Virgin in
the window will not be harmed.*

fortable and contented, the people of Chartres had few complaints.

Chartres prospered with the times. The last twelfth-century Bishop of Chartres, Renaud de Mouçon, had no patience with even commonplace inefficiency. Renaud was a magnificent warrior—he had been a hero in the otherwise ill-fated Third Crusade (1188–1192), led by his friend and rival, England's lionhearted king, Richard I—and he quickly reinforced the city's fortifications. Merchants abroad, who might have felt that Chartres' apparent vulnerability to disaster was now a thing of the past, were attracted to the commercial center, ensuring the economic future of the town. Using his prestige and imposing reputation to good advantage, Renaud reformed the administrative setup, purged corrupt elements, introduced economies that made the prospering town more prosperous still, and brightened already bright prospects. Chartres, it seemed early in the last decade of the twelfth century, was a flawless place.

If it was flawless, it was not so for long. On the tenth day of June, 1194, fire broke out, its origins unknown. For

two days the most furious flames in the charred history of the city lapped and leveled everything in their path. Most of the town was destroyed and with it the cathedral, except for the foundation and crypt and Chartres West, the Royal Portal, which were made of stone.

The people of Chartres knew what was expected of them. They would be in understandable mourning for a while—but not for too long: Chartrains were practical people. Soon, they knew, they would do as their ancestors had done and put body, soul, and pocketbook into the construction of a new palace of the Virgin, finer and more glorious than any built before. That was the way it was supposed to be in Chartres. Past generations had made the traditions that the present generation followed—all the while outdoing past generations in a competitive burst of energy.

This time, however, the mourning lingered, and the spirits of the Chartrains wilted day after day instead of rallying. The tradition seemed ended; the reason: the sacred tunic. Through fire and theft, through disasters manmade and natural, the red garment had endured for nearly three centuries. It had become the symbol—more than a symbol, the tangible proof—of the Virgin's presence within the sanctuary. Now that it was gone, rebuilding would be foolhardy: the cathedral only would burn again. The people were convinced that their sins—and in the Middle Ages the simple enjoyment of good times could be interpreted as sinfulness—had so infuriated the Holy Mother that she had departed from her special palace, allowing it and her tunic to perish.

Hearing the tragic news of the fire, Cardinal Melior of Pisa, the papal legate (or ambassador from the Pope) in France, hastened to the town. He needed only to walk around for a few minutes to see how extensive was the damage. A perceptive man, he realized that the most serious damage had affected not the cathedral or the town— they could be rebuilt—but the spirit of the people. Their will to exist as a community seemed to be gone, and their melancholy seemed to deepen day by day. Conferring with Bishop Renaud, the cardinal argued that the cathedral must be rebuilt before the spiritual damage was beyond repair.

The bishop and the chapter (the officers of the diocese) agreed; they even pledged to invest the greater part of the diocese's revenue in the reconstruction for at least the following three years. But they remained skeptical. They

Constructed early in the twelfth century, the crypt of Bishop Fulbert (left) survived the fire of 1194, which proved so destructive to the Cathedral of Chartres.

knew that the people could be pressed into service but that their hearts would not be in their work. What good was the cathedral without the relic? No good, they knew the people were thinking. And without a meaningful cathedral, the town of Chartres would not function as it had. The cardinal, however, promised to take care of the morale problem.

On the next feast day in Chartres the dispirited people gathered apathetically at the ashen site of the cathedral for services. That Cardinal Melior would officiate was virtually a command for one hundred per cent attendance. After celebrating Mass, the Italian addressed the assembly. We cannot know what he said, but it seems reasonable to assume that his sermon was extremely moving; he was, after all, an ambassador from the Pope, and he was well known as an eloquent and melodramatic speaker.

Melior undoubtedly reminded them of the importance of Chartres Cathedral to all Christendom; he must have pleaded for its reconstruction; he must have recalled the

95

traditions of the edifice and its builders and projected gloomily a future without a great church. All this must have moved the Chartrians to tears, and if they thought of the lost tunic, they probably wept openly. Finally—perhaps just when the sermon was becoming at once most dramatic and most painful—Bishop Renaud and the chapter appeared in procession. As the people turned to look, they saw, at the head of the procession, a familiar fold of red; the priests came closer; they were indeed carrying it—the sacred relic itself.

As the mood changed abruptly from deep gloom to exhilaration, Cardinal Melior explained simply that the tunic had been safely locked away in the cathedral crypt. In the immediate aftermath of the fire, whoever had placed it there had forgotten that he had done so. The people realized that they had misunderstood. The Holy Mother had not punished them. She only wanted them to know that she desired a newer, grander church erected as her palace. Immediately coins and jewels and furs and pledges of more fell in a torrent of giving before the passage of the sacred tunic. They would build the shrine that she had asked them for; they would make it worthy of her. They would do their ancestors proud—and they would outdo their ancestors as well. The civic determination that took shape that day never faltered until the brilliant new cathedral was completed in 1220.

The merchants of Chartres were instrumental in seeing to it that the initial enthusiasm never failed. The future of their businesses, they understood, depended on the reconstruction of the cathedral. As a perceptive medieval scribe once wrote, "The temple has always attracted the merchant just because it attracts the faithful. . . . There is no feast without its fair, no fair without its feast: one calls for the other." Thus the businessmen gave generously, and in prudently distributed installments to keep the building going and to prevent their donations from being exhausted on an overly lavish beginning.

A contemporary writer mentioned that beginning with the reappearance of the garment, a number of miracles were "achieved." Whether God or the chapter or Cardinal

Opposite, the west façade of Chartres Cathedral. The three main portals, the windows above them, and the south (right) spire date from the twelfth century; the rose window, from the thirteenth. One of Europe's most beautiful structures in its own right, the north spire was built in the 1500's.

Melior was responsible, the miraculous achievements were sung about from Germany to Italy and inspired a continual inflow of pilgrims to Chartres and an unending supply of volunteer labor.

There was the miracle of the child beggar Guillot, an orphan whose tongue had been cut out by a vicious knight. Journeying to busy Chartres to beg for his bread, Guillot knelt before the charred altar of the Virgin in prayer. Suddenly, the tongueless child erupted in articulate prayers of praise that amazed all present. Word of the miracle—a boy with no tongue praying with the eloquence of a poet—spread quickly. But by the time the pilgrims who traveled to Chartres arrived to see him, little Guillot had received a new tongue, a gift from the Holy Mother and another miracle.

Then there was an English student, on his way home from Paris, penniless. Stopping at Soissons en route, he heard a sermon by a visiting priest from Chartres. Like all present, the poor Englishman was moved by the stories of misfortune in Chartres, but when the collection came around to him, he had no money to give. He did, however, have a golden necklace, which he had purchased at great sacrifice in Paris as a gift for his sweetheart in London; and this precious jewelry he gave to the Chartres building fund. That night, asleep in a barn, the young student was awakened by heavenly light and found himself confronted by three beautiful women. One of them said that she was the Lady of Chartres, and she returned his necklace to him. Vowing to dedicate his life to her, the Englishman returned home, said good-by to his family (and no doubt to his girl friend), and retired to a desert island, where he lived the rest of his life as a holy hermit.

This story miraculously moved the lion's heart of King Richard. Although he was at the time at war with Philippe-Auguste of France, Richard guaranteed safe passage to all bound for Chartres. He sent donations to the town and retained a lifelong admiration for the cathedral, which he often visited, war or no war.

There were unexplained torches that illuminated the road to Chartres on moonless nights, loaves of bread that were eaten in the afternoon and that reappeared in ovens in the evening, and even a prison break engineered by Providence to enable an incarcerated fuel merchant to transport oil to Chartres to light the lamps of the cathedral.

Thus, no conscription was necessary, no prodding was needed; everyone present was willing—eager—to participate. Pilgrims, serfs, laborers, farmers, craftsmen, merchants, masons—all worked together in as nearly a classless environment as was possible in the Middle Ages. Since everyone involved felt a personal interest in the new cathedral, everyone had his own ideas about where this or that ought to go, how big such-and-such should be, and so forth. This made things more difficult for the master mason. He had to be a competent diplomat as well as a brilliant mason.

That he was a brilliant mason is all that is known for certain about the master of Chartres. Until recently, many scholars thought that there were three masters, each more or less equally responsible for the completed structure. Today, however, more are beginning to accept the idea that the first master was the principal one. It is probable that he had almost complete control over the design and construction of the edifice, for Bishop Renaud, proud warrior that he was, was also a most practical administrator. He wanted the cathedral rebuilt quickly, and knowing little about architecture himself, he very likely hired a mason of proven ability, to whom he delegated all responsibility.

In fact, almost everyone connected with the building of Chartres Cathedral must have had a remarkable power of restraint, despite circumstances that seemed to dictate lavishness. The mason was in virtually complete command, a situation that generally encouraged displays of virtuosity. He had a willing construction crew and more than enough funds. The cathedral crusade had reached the peak at which it would be maintained for many years to come, and the splendid Cathedral of Notre Dame in Paris, then under construction only fifty miles away, must have provided an incentive to compete.

Yet, with all this, with all the circumstances conducive to the construction of a more elaborate church, the Cathedral of Chartres rose modestly, almost austerely. For this the master mason undoubtedly was largely responsible, but the other workers, skilled and unskilled, must have felt similarly restrained. Perhaps they all realized that the Chartrain tradition called for a dignified, humble sanctuary in keeping with the character of the Lady whose spiritual home it was supposed to be.

Because it is uncluttered by superfluous detail, the Cathedral of Chartres is a good subject for a study of Gothic structural systems. And because so much of the earlier edifices remains underneath and within the building, the cathedral also provides illustrations of the structural principles from which the Gothic sprang.

The basic basilican plan of the Cathedral of Chartres was established when the nave and choir were built early in the eleventh century. After that Romanesque structure burned down, its foundation was re-used, and the layout remained. With the addition of the transepts in the twelfth century, Chartres assumed the cross-shaped basilican plan that characterized many Gothic cathedrals.

The master of Chartres worked directly over the crypt of Bishop Fulbert's church, and so his layout was already determined. This was not much of a limitation, though. In the first place, the arrangement was with very few exceptions the only one employed in west European church building after the tenth century: the basilican plan. Secondly, like all Gothic structures, the Cathedral of Chartres was designed and erected vertically.

The basilican plan was usually but not necessarily cruciform, or cross-shaped, with the section beyond the intersection a semicircle. This rounded protrusion, called the *apse*, characteristically was divided into a *choir* in the center and an *ambulatory*, a circular corridor that surrounded the choir. A series of small chapels was built off the ambulatory. The apse generally faced eastward, toward the Holy Land. Extending away from the apse toward the west was the longest section of the cross shape: the *nave*, where the congregation gathered. Defined by a parallel double row of columns, the nave was flanked by *aisles*. The *transept* was the shorter section of the cross, perpendicular to the nave. The area where the nave and transept intersected was named, appropriately enough, the *crossing*. Portals or entrances were constructed at either end of the transept, and the main portal was at the end of the nave—the west façade. At Chartres the west portal of Bishop Geoffrey was spared in the great fire of 1194.

To understand the verticality of Gothic architecture, we might look beyond the Middle Ages to an earlier time when building principles were formed but techniques were not yet so complicated.

Early civilizations developed two ways of building, and

until modern times these two systems, or combinations of both, have provided the basis for almost all construction. Where stone and good timber were readily available—in Mycenaean Greece, for example—people placed horizontal elements (roofs, ceilings) on the vertical elements (walls, columns) that acted as supports. This system is called *post-and-lintel*. On the other hand, nomadic peoples and such peoples as the Mesopotamians, whose muddy, marshy land afforded little or no stone and timber, developed the system known as *vaulting*. In its most primitive expression, a vault might be a double row of tapered reeds placed firmly in the ground, their tops bent toward each other and tied. Then leaves and mud, or skins, or thinner reeds could be placed

A stylized elevation of Chartres Cathedral indicates the distribution of space inside the recognizably Gothic edifice. Capped by a pointed timber roof and supported by external flying buttresses, the vaulted nave is the highest point in the interior and is flanked by vaulted aisles. Above the aisles, at the triforium level, are open passageways formed by the floor and vaulted roofing.

over the vault. The vault most familiar to Americans is the Indian wigwam.

The structural basis behind each system is completely different from that of the other. Post-and-lintel is an equal balance of horizontal and vertical forces; the skeleton of a post-and-lintel building and the shell are the same thing. The vault, on the other hand, is a purely vertical structure, its arches always exerting downward-outward pressure (in architecture called *thrust*); a vaulted building is constructed from the inside outward, the vault itself being nothing more than a skeleton around which any shell might be built.

Many Romanesque churches had vaulted naves under timber roofs of post-and-lintel construction. Within the nave parallel rows of columns were built, and round arches were erected across the nave from each column to the column opposite. This series of round arches produced the half-cylinder shape appropriately called the barrel or tunnel vault. By that time, needless to say, reed and mud had been left far behind: the Romanesque vaults were made of tapered stone blocks placed over arch skeletons of timber. The heaviness of the stone greatly increased the natural thrust peculiar to all vaulted structures. To prevent the thrust of the vaults from pushing the walls of the church downward and outward from their tops, the builders braced the walls from the outside with vertical supporting elements known as *buttresses*.

When the old structure at Chartres burned down, the master mason was determined to replace it with a church that would incorporate all the more up-to-date elements that had been perfected in the second half of the twelfth century—the elements of the Gothic.

Where columns had been, the master ordered the erection of *piers*—clusters of slender pillars that emphasized the verticality of the interior. Put up by the cutters of hardstone, who carefully joined matched cylinders of stone, the piers not only provided the basic skeleton around which the cathedral would take shape, but they also were useful as cores to which scaffolding could be fastened. When the piers were finished, they were joined by arches; but now, instead of building round arches from one pillar to its op-

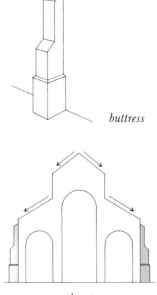

buttress

thrust

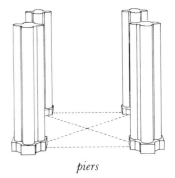

piers

Sunlit in the background of the picture of Chartres (opposite) are the thick, cylindrical columns commonly used in church building before the Gothic era. In the left foreground are the characteristically Gothic clustered piers—tall, slender, and well suited to the verticality of the style.

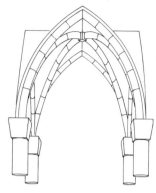

ribbed vault

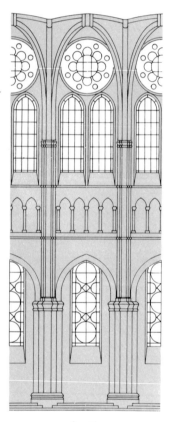

elevation

posite, the workmen erected much larger round arches across the nave from one pier to the one diagonally across from it.

Each set of four piers, forming a square or rectangle called a *bay*, was therefore crisscrossed by a pair of round arches. Since the diameter of a square is half again as long as the side, the diagonal arches were much higher than the arches along each side of the bay. To eliminate the awkward look of disproportionate arches at the sides, masons began to make the side-to-side arches pointed to the height of the diagonal arch. This sort of vault was called a *ribbed vault*, and it was very important to the development of the Gothic; it permitted masons to build much higher than they ever had before.

The ribbed vault was the skeleton of the Gothic cathedral. Its majestic elevation made larger windows possible and was responsible for the brilliant illumination of the interior. But to preserve this quality, the workers had to build out from and around the skeleton in a way that would not neutralize the openness gained by the ribbed vault.

At Our Lady of Chartres and many other cathedrals of the era, the elevation was three stories. Some churches were divided into only two stories, and others into four. But a three-step *elevation* was more conventional.

The first level rose to about half the total height of the vault, and this level, or *arcade*, determined the height of the outer walls of the cathedral. The tops of the arcade level and the outer walls were joined by planks, making a useful platform for the workers and later a roof for the aisles. Level two, about fourteen feet high and therefore the smallest, was the *triforium*. Timber was extended from the top of the triforium to the top of the outer walls, where it joined the aisle roof and formed a triangular passageway within the church at the triforium level. The rest of the elevated vault had nothing outside it but the sun and the sky. Fittingly called the *clearstory*, this uppermost level let in the precious light; the higher it soared, the higher soared the admiration of the people.

The greatly increased height of the Gothic ribbed vault over that of its Romanesque predecessor created one major problem, however. Since the outer walls of the church were

On a bright, sunny day, Chartres from the inside appears to be the most delicate of all cathedrals—a mere outline of a building within colored light. At right, light illuminates the tripartite elevation of Chartres.

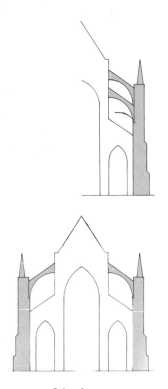

flying buttress

generally no higher than the triforium, the buttresses built against them could not counter the thrust of the higher vault. The solution was the *flying buttress*, which was used on a massive scale for the first time at the Cathedral of Notre Dame in Paris. It was simply an arched support extending from the regular buttress in a gentle curve to the high walls of the ribbed vault.

An interesting idea about the possible original purpose of the flying buttress has been causing some controversy among historians in recent decades. Some scholars now maintain that the flying buttress was meant as nothing more than a temporary shoring device. They suggest that the first flying buttresses at Notre Dame were placed against the vault to counter the thrust while the mortar was setting (which could take as long as two years) and that the masons intended to remove them later. But when the time came, the theorists speculate, the masons hesitated, unwilling to take the chance that set mortar alone would hold up the church. Giving the idea some credibility is the fact that early flying buttresses were not decorated as were the other parts of the cathedrals. The master of Chartres was, in fact, the first mason to decorate the flying buttresses as though they belonged to the overall design.

With the addition of a pointed wooden roof, the Cathedral of Our Lady of Chartres was finished. The structure, as mentioned earlier, was unusually restrained. Decoration on the column capitals was spare and simple; the clustered piers rose straight and unembellished; the stone was dressed and polished to a soft luster, but not to the high sheen favored in more ostentatious cathedrals. And yet Chartres Cathedral could be described as meager by no sensible person. Even from a distance the edifice is imposing, with its unmatched spires soaring high over the roofs of the town. (The southern tower on Chartres West was erected sometime between 1145 and 1170 and survived the 1194 fire. The northern spire, taller and more ornate, was added in the sixteenth century.) Its north and south transept portals are unusually large and are dramatically decorated with big sculptured figures, although it is the older statuary on Chartres West that has remained the most widely admired sculpture in the structure. Apparently the basic work was completed in 1210, and because there must have been so much money left over and so many workers still anxious to make a contribution, the master mason took ten more years and added porches lengthwise along the north and south sides of the nave.

Inside there are niches with statues, painted and mosaic panels, screens, fine wood carving, rich tapestries, jeweled vestments and vessels, golden candlesticks, and a wide variety of tastefully decorated elements. Yet the visitor to Chartres Cathedral conceivably could notice none of them. For it is not statuary that brings out whatever religious feelings the visitor might have concealed. It is not painting or the finely cut gem that makes the pious worshipful, the respectful pious, and the atheist respectful. It is not the tapestry that bathes the interior in a colorful light so pure and exquisite that it seems to have arrived straight from heaven, somehow spared the dulling journey through space, air, and clouds.

It is glass.

It is glass that has drawn people to Chartres for eight hundred years, glass that moved the poet James Russell Lowell to write:

> I gaze round on the windows, pride of France!
> Each the bright gift of some mechanic guild,
> Who loved their city and thought gold well spent
> To make her beautiful with piety.

As though complementing—instead of competing with—the splendid stained glass windows, most of the stonework of the Cathedral of Chartres is slender and airy. Elegant in their simplicity, the flying buttresses (left) are less ornate than those that usually are characteristic of Gothic buildings.

VI

VOICES OF THE CATHEDRAL

Master Clement stood in the Chapel of All Saints at the new Cathedral of Chartres, shouting orders to his apprentices as they measured and made diagrams of the window. Alongside and perhaps slightly behind the famous glass painter hovered a shoemaker. Hanging onto every word, nodding from time to time, squinting as he glanced up to see what the helpers were doing, the shoemaker tried very hard to look as though he understood what was going on, as though he were confirming each of Clement's directives. But in fact, he never had been more confused in his life: it was all a mystery to him.

He represented the shoemakers' guild, which—sometime after 1210—had commissioned the great Clement to create a stained glass window depicting the story of Saint Martin. A smaller window below would show shoemakers at work. The pair would be the guild's donation to the cathedral, and the shoemakers were quite nervous about it. Although all of Chartres's guilds were donating windows, not all had gone to the extravagance of hiring a master of Clement's caliber. Nevertheless, if human nature in the Middle Ages was not too radically different from what it has been in all other ages, the representative that the shoemakers had elected set the membership's mind at ease at the next guild meeting.

Things were coming along very nicely, he might have told them. Oh, Clement almost had made a disastrous blunder, but he, the shoemaker, had caught it in time, and everything was all right now. The members must have been relieved, and the next day and frequently thereafter they probably found that their duties somehow took them right

Opposite, two stained glass windows—one picturing Saint Foy, the other the Virgin and Jesus—at Chartres Cathedral. On this page, the cobblers occupy one of many windows that recorded the contribution of local guilds.

by the Chapel of All Saints, where they might have stopped for a chat with the patient Clement.

The shoemakers' guild, edgy as its membership was, was grateful for the opportunity to invest its money in the window. Their donation at last bound them visibly to the community energy that was the real master builder of Chartres.

The shoemakers, of course, always had been bound to it. As in any successful crusade, military or otherwise, progress was largely dependent on civilian manpower not directly involved in the campaign. The hordes of laborers needed shoes to work in, and the shoemakers not only had to double their output at least, but also had to make the shoes tougher than usual. Similarly, weavers were required virtually to mass-produce the garments worn and so quickly worn out by the workers. While stuffing their ovens with thrice the loaves of bread normally baked, the bakers had to sacrifice none of the richness and wholesomeness. Money-changers, tavern keepers, wine makers, blacksmiths, grocers, apothecaries, furriers, tanners, cobblers— all were prospering from the traffic brought to Chartres by the rebuilding of the cathedral; and all no doubt had the blisters and the fatigue-ringed eyes to show for it.

Although the town's craftsmen were essential to the progress of rebuilding, they were not happy that their participation was so indirect. The cook knew perfectly well that his hearty meals were keeping the workmen well fed and energetic, that their efficiency therefore reflected his, that he had every right to take a personal pride in the cathedral. But then in a melancholy moment he might ask himself what stones, timber, or tiles he could point to and identify as his own. None at all, he would answer; all he was doing was getting rich from the rebuilding of the palace of the Holy Virgin, Our Lady of Chartres.

Guild meetings, the group therapy sessions of their time, gave members the opportunity to air all their problems, professional and personal, in confidence. The subject of the role their trade was playing in the rebuilding of the cathedral must have been discussed at several meetings, but which guild first decided to immortalize its profession

Above, left, the window of the wine carriers' guild. Opposite, the rose window and three "lancet" windows at Chartres. The Tree of Jesse is the subject of the left lancet; the life of Christ is condensed in the center; and scenes from the Passion and Resurrection are depicted on the right.

110

with a stained glass window is not known. In any case, it was a perfect solution. For one thing, while the making of stained glass was an ancient craft, it really had flourished only when the heavy-walled Romanesque churches, with their small, narrow windows, had been overtaken by the high-vaulted Gothic. The colored windows were in great demand and were very expensive. For another, the noblemen who had been donating stained glass windows to the cathedrals had begun the practice of having their own images represented on smaller windows beneath the large ones; thus the guild had a precedent to cite when it asked that the profession of its members be immortalized in glass.

Once the first two or three guild windows were installed, the other guilds could not resist the temptation to compete. Ironically, the masons, sculptors, carpenters, smiths, and other groups working directly on the building also took up collections and paid for a window, usually for several. Even the lowly water carriers' guild—which, for all we know, might have been formed exclusively for the purpose of donating a window—contributed a chapel window. Rather touchingly, the members had their bent, bucket-bearing bodies represented in glass beneath their donation, a depiction of the life of Saint Mary Magdalene. The knights, counts, and other prosperous people elsewhere depicted look pompous and unholy by comparison.

Many of the windows seem equally fitting. The first missionary, Saint Paul, relives his life in glass for all to see, while below, the basketmakers fashion their baskets just as openly. Ezekiel, David, and an angel look down from the clearstory; under them the butchers trim the meat. While

E. FIEVET, CHARTRES

GIRAUDON

E. FIEVET, CHARTRES

E. FIEVET, CHARTRES

Pictured on these pages are some of the windows at Chartres that record the donations of the local guilds. At left is the window of the fabric dealers. Above, top, the water-bearers; center, leather tanners; bottom, furriers. Right, the blacksmiths and wheelwrights; and at far right, the carpenters.

the Virgin prepares to receive the Magi, the bakers display their bread. The same bakers prepare some loaves under the figure of Moses, who, of course, went for forty years without tasting or even seeing a loaf of bread—a little medieval joke, no doubt.

The result, therefore, of this tornado of professional generosity was a cathedral with one hundred seventy-five magnificent stained glass windows. Naturally, reports of the windows raced across Europe, and the competitive bishops began sending for the glass painters of Chartres or sending their own glass painters there to study the windows. In consequence, the thirteenth century saw a profusion of lovely windows appear along with the profusion of new cathedrals. The work at Chartres, however, never was equaled: the most beautiful stained glass windows when they were installed, they have remained the most beautiful stained glass windows in the world.

Paradoxically, after developing for a hundred years or so, the art of stained glass achieved a level of technical perfection that ultimately caused a decline of artistry. When Master Clement went to work for the shoemakers' guild, he used methods that had changed little from those used by the ancient Egyptians; and these methods worked beautifully. To color the glass, Clement had to sandwich raw pigment between sheets of crude, unevenly blown, bubbly glass and bake the conglomeration until the color was sealed into the glass: he had no way of knowing how much color would take and how much would melt away. To cut the glass to size, he used a clumsy hot iron that likely as not would curl the edges and streak the sheet. To vary the tex-

Before they reach their earthly destination, sunrays must travel millions of miles. If their destination is Chartres, a finishing touch is added just as the journey is about to end: the stained glass windows bathe the rays in color before they can strike the floor.

ture, he applied acids to the glass without knowing precisely what effect the acids would have on the colors. But these very haphazard and primitive techniques produced the most marvelous glass—glass that seemingly was determined to be an obstacle to the rays of the sun. Its streaks, curls, bubbles, stains, and scars could not stop the powerful light, but they could slow it down, change it, and let it pass into the cathedral more beautiful than it had been during its long trip earthward.

A visitor at Chartres, standing in one place and turning himself slowly around, can experience a world of light and color. The pale golden yellow of a sunrise and the vivid white of noontime on the ocean; the brilliant orange-red of a reluctant sunset and the silver blues of twilight; the misty, filtered light of fog; the sharply defined rays, almost separated one by one, of sunlight making its way through the umbrellas of a forest, choosing just this or that to illuminate on the foliaged floor—all the light and color present at some place some time every day on earth are present all at once at Chartres, thanks to the imperfect glass of the windows.

Gradually—and unfortunately—the technique was perfected. In large workshops well staffed with assistants, the artists learned to use heat and pressure to tint the glass evenly. They ironed out the bubbles and kept the edges from curling, removed the scars and made the glass smooth and transparent. Master Clement, despite his title of glass painter, had used paint very sparingly (at the most for the features of a face and the buttons of a coat). His successors complained that they had no time to assemble scraps of colored glass, and they began to fill in more and more of the details in translucent paint over the tinted backgrounds. But the perfected glass did not challenge the sun; and the sun, in turn, ignored it and passed right through it as though it were not there at all.

The age of the great stained glass windows was short, but its fruits were bountiful; and the extraordinary care that the people of Europe have lavished on the fragile masterpieces has preserved a remarkably high percentage of them. Threatened by Nazi invasion in the late 1930's, the citizens of the major cathedral towns of France and Belgium removed the glass, piece by piece, from the window casings, wrapped the sections individually, and stored them in secret places known to only a few: thus were the precious windows of the Gothic saved from the Gothlike onrush of the Germans. That the people were so conscientious is one of history's happier happenings—not only because the windows are so rare and beautiful, but also because stained glass windows are unique phenomena in art.

Of what other kind of visual art can it be said: The beauty of the object attracts attention before the object itself does. Indeed, the visitor to the Cathedral of Chartres does not even have to look at the stained glass windows to see how beautiful they are. Entering the edifice for the first time, for instance, he might find his attention drawn to the wood carving of the altar. Admiring the rainbow throbbing within the deep burnished browns, he soon would realize that the prismatic colors did not originate in the wood but were being reflected in it. Even his own skin would be tattooed with the shimmering lights. Unless he closed his eyes, he could not help but see the art of the windows, even if for some reason he deliberately avoided looking at the windows themselves.

Casting their unifying light over all the cathedral's parts, the stained glass windows were the choirmasters of the church, imposing their outlook on all the parts, but blending them all into the whole interior structure. Still, there were other parts, other kinds of decoration, each with its own story to tell in its own voice. And like the windows (which were for all their intrusiveness the most eloquent voices of the cathedral), the others were articulate and educational, which was only proper, since the cathedral was to many people in the Middle Ages the only education that they ever would have.

· Like the art of stained glass, the art of tapestry weaving reached a peak in the Western world during the cathedral crusade; and like the windows, the tapestries were decorated with stories of the saints and prophets, although their basic purpose was a structural one.

The interiors of the Gothic cathedrals had no walls separating one section from another. While the resulting vast spaciousness was considered an artistic virtue, it did not always lend itself to the many special rites and ceremonies and meetings held in the cathedral. Heavy hanging tapestries provided the solution: they could be stored in the crypt and removed according to need—hauled outdoors to decorate civil ceremonies, presented to visiting kings as gifts, used even as road markers, then hung across the nave again to separate the meeting of the tanners' guild from that of the wheelwrights. When a storm blew up, the tapestries were hung inside the portals and did an efficient job of keeping out drafts.

A peculiarly Gothic style of tapestry developed somewhat later than did other forms of Gothic art. The reason for this was that big woven rugs did not appear in Europe until the crusaders brought them back from the Middle East. There were some monks who had learned to operate looms, but certainly not with the expertise required to work on the scale of the Islamic tapestries. Weavers and drapers knew something about the technical end of the weaving process, but their specialty had been the manufacture and tailoring of fabrics: from their trade to that of the tapestry weaver's was a formidable leap. (The relationship between the trades was something like the relationship between the carpenter and the cabinetmaker, or to take a more extreme example, like that of the house painter to the portrait painter.)

The thirteenth century, then, was a period of learning in western European weavers' guilds. The first presentable

tapestries that came out of the workshops were patterned with simple geometric shapes; early in the 1300's the symbols of heraldry began to appear on heavy rugs that were carried as though they were banners by three or four men at the head of a lord's entourage. Small animals and birds soon made their way into the warp and woof of the weave, but progress was very slow, one reason being the reluctance of the weavers to experiment. To correct a mistake in a tapestry was a monumental job, often requiring the unraveling of much or all of the rug.

In the decade between 1360 and 1370 the weaving art

Above, an angel sounds the second trumpet in one of a series of magnificent fourteenth-century Angers (France) tapestries depicting The Apocalypse.

abruptly broke into a mad dash and caught up with the Gothic age. The sudden emergence of artistic excellence represented the culmination of the trend toward large, well-organized workshops that had been developing in the fourteenth century. Even by the standards of our age of technology, the medieval tapestry workshops—especially in northern France and Flanders—were highly industrialized operations, employing both fabric weavers and artists, establishing if not assembly-line at least mass-production techniques.

The *tapissiers* (tapestry weavers) apparently were willing to experiment for a number of years and considered the money lost an investment. They developed charting systems so that any of the many standard weaves could be reproduced identically each and every time it was called for. And most important of all, the workshop *tapissiers* replaced the old patterns and simple figures of creatures with handsome scenes depicting Bible stories, knights in battle, landscapes, troops of minstrels, or *genre* (concerned with everyday life, such as a kitchen or tavern scene). At the very beginning most of the pictures were copied from old illuminated manuscripts, but before long the weavers began to design their own pictures.

The response to the new tapestries was phenomenal. Because the rugs were so extremely expensive, the ostentatious aristocracy loved them, collected them, and on their travels took them with them in specially designed wagons so that all could see their wealth. King Charles V of France, his three jealous brothers, and the legion of aristocratic hangers-on that this particular royal family attracted all scattered from Paris to Flanders to find *tapissiers* to weave more and better tapestries for them than for anyone else. The demand was too great for most of the workshops to handle, and that, as matters developed, was a blessing.

Caught up in the fad for collecting, the supercilious, tasteless courtiers around Charles V avidly sought the rare and the expensive. The beauty of an object was to many of them immaterial: if a thing looked costly, it was worth owning. After the initial impressiveness of the figured tapestries wore off, the nobles began bringing pressure to bear on the workshops to design richer-looking rugs—perhaps some golden thread here, a tighter weave all over, more detail there, and so forth. Two centuries later, when times were bad and the tapestry business had fallen off, the weavers would give in, try to make their tapestries look like paintings, and destroy their art. But, fortunately, at this dawn of a brilliant era for the art, business was so good that the *tapissier* could afford to be independent. In fact, the prudent patron did not argue too strongly for fear of offending the artist and having him refuse the commission altogether.

For reasons that are rather vague, the tapestries in the great cathedrals tend to deal less with religious subjects than do the windows and the sculpture. It may have been that the tapestries were donated by noblemen who preferred secular subjects.

The most famous workshop in Europe was at Arras in northern France. So closely was it associated with tapestry that in England *arras* became and remains a synonym for tapestry, as is *arazzi* in Italian and *Panas de ras* in Spanish.

Regretfully, only one certain set of Arras tapestry remains, and it is incomplete. Commissioned for the Cathedral of Tournai—which is in Belgium now, although it used to belong to France—this tapestry tells the story of St. Piat and St. Eleuthere, who are clothed in fourteenth-century apparel, not in the third- and sixth-century garments that the saints really wore. All of the scenes are, in fact, treated as everyday events. The style of weaving represents the craft at its Gothic best. The weave itself is loose, the figures are flat and unmodeled. Architectural elements and figures are grouped closely together, almost overcrowded, while relatively empty space remains elsewhere. Such composition is commonplace in tapestry, for the *tapissier* was interested in preserving, not in concealing, the flat rug quality of the tapestry: thus he created patterns with the figures.

Tournai had its own famous workshop, which was Arras' foremost competitor. Their styles were quite similar, however, and the two shops occasionally collaborated on large projects.

The portable tapestries were unpredictable: one day a woven unicorn might have kept out the drafts; the next day Saint Francis feeding the birds might have watched over the pastry cooks' guild as its members discussed the rising cost of sugar.

Along with stained glass windows, tapestries in the great cathedrals were the artistic counterpart of mural paintings in the buildings of later ages. Inasmuch as the Gothic style was essentially architectural in character —its parts always serving the cause of design unity— the windows and tapestries assumed decorative roles only after they had established functional ones. They were

rennement list la creuesh
de Rems ❡ Apres seoit
lempereur ❡ Apres seoit
le Roy Ambledure en milieu
du front de la sale ❡ Apres
le Roy de france seoit le roy

des romains · Et auoit autant de distance
du· Roy au Roy des romains côme du
Roy a lempereur· Et auoient lempereur
le Roy et le Roy des romains chascun se
parement ou ciel de drap dor tyrre de velin
au aus armes de france· et par dessus ceulx

architectural elements in a way that paintings on walls could not be.

Painting was, however, a highly developed, widely practiced art during the Gothic era. As the illustrations throughout this book indicate, the monastic scribes who made the beautiful illuminated manuscripts of the Middle Ages were skilled and sensitive painters.

Gothic sculpture achieved the greatest harmony with Gothic architecture. As did the churches, it changed significantly from what it had been a century before, and it had changed drastically from the way it had been in the tenth century. The flattened, angular torsos of the chiseled bodies had become rounder and more supple. Hair, which in the Romanesque period had been represented by circles knotted tightly against heads, had begun to loosen and fall free. Robes that formerly had been ribbed cylinders almost had begun to ripple on the Gothic statuary. Invariably round eyes had turned into variable, expressive, almond-shaped eyes, and little smiles had begun to appear on lips of stone. Bodies joined immovably to stone niches had begun to break away.

Day by day during the cathedral crusade, sculptors became more skillful: their figures were more lifelike than any had been since the Classical Age—and more impatient, too, more independent, anxious to free themselves from the confinement of being relief sculpture. (Almost no free-standing sculpture—sculpture in the round, as it usually is called—was created in the Middle Ages. Moreover, virtually all figures still were painted with bright colors, as statues always had been. Not until the Renaissance would unpainted stone become conventional for sculpture.)

The sculpture on Gothic cathedrals did a great deal to provide the stability that medieval people—that almost any people in any time—liked to be able to depend on in a

In the manuscript illustration opposite, King Charles V of France and his royal guests seem impervious to the battle raging beside their banquet. A better patron of the arts than head of state, Charles spent a fortune on such tapestries as the German one at right. The patterned background and the flatness of the figures were typical of Gothic-style weaving in the fourteenth century.

*Characteristic of Gothic cathedrals, the tympanum above the central portal
of the west façade of Bourges was decorated with a relief depicting* The
Last Judgment, *above. The figures were carved between 1240 and 1250.*

place they visited often. The Parisian who habitually entered the Cathedral of Notre Dame through the Portal of St. Anne did not have to look each time to know that the kings and priests flanking the door were glaring at him as he went in; whether he looked or did not look, he was glad to know that the Virgin enthroned high up in the center of the tympanum with Jesus on her lap was there as usual, presiding as the story of her life was told in bas-relief all around her. Leaving through the Portal of the Last Judgment, he did not have to look back to see the thin but dominant figure of Jesus judging; he did not have to check to see if the images of heaven were still on Christ's right, hell on his left. The images of the pious and stern-looking prophets on the heaven side were implanted in him, and he did not have to remind himself not to laugh instead of recoiling in horror at the grotesque demons and gargoyles on the hell side: he would not look at all. But he still would be glad that they were all there.

They were all there—all the people whose lives touched him: the God he worshiped; the saints who intrigued him; the bishops and lords who protected him, as they put it, or who beat him down, as he put it, or who exploited him, as we might put it. The knights whom he probably hated were represented somewhere, as well as the merchants and craftsmen whom he envied, and the people with whom he worked, and the beggars whom he was not likely to pity. Perhaps the sheep that he herded or the fox that he had been trying to trap were there too: the sculpture of the Gothic cathedral neglected no one.

Gothic sculpture differed from the Romanesque in tone as well as in style. In the depictions of the Last Judgment, a favorite subject for cathedral portals, the possibility of salvation rather than damnation began to dominate. Symbols of the liberal arts indicated that salvation could be achieved through the pursuit of knowledge—not, as before, simply through unquestioning obedience to Church law as interpreted by the priesthood. The Second Coming of Christ was heralded, and whereas before he had been a stern judge, fair but aloof and majestic, he now was becoming a more human-looking, compassionate teacher, seemingly eager to forgive, to help, to teach. The Old

OVERLEAF: *On the later Gothic cathedrals, almost all exposed exterior surfaces were decorated with relief sculpture. These graceful, pleasant-looking figures flank a portal at the Cathedral of Strasbourg in France.*

BOTH: JEAN ROUBIER

123

Testament, long neglected, began to take a greater role in providing the subject matter of the reliefs. One of the most meaningful changes was in the posture of the sculpted figures. In Romanesque sculpture the saints are stiff and look straight out and down from their niches, sometimes glaring threateningly at the assembly. The Gothic figures, in contrast, turn toward one another and toward the congregation, as though they were sympathetically discussing the people among themselves. This, to a certain extent, stressed the value of personal relationships and the importance of dialogue in the decision-making processes of life.

Since the earliest days of Christian church building, the stone calendar—usually placed inside the edifice, near the main portal—had been especially meaningful to the peasant. At first the calendars were simple and simply carved illustrations of the months and seasons, but in the Gothic era they became bigger and more beautiful. In some churches the peasants themselves, with the help of a mason, were charged with executing the sculpture. The handsomest and most famous stone cathedral calendar is the huge circular one at the Cathedral of Amiens.

January was a month for feasting: in the first wedge of a typical calendar a family is shown seated around a bountiful table, reading, radiating happiness. In February's section the family might be sitting around a fire, looking less happy, although winter provisions—at Amiens, a ham hanging from the ceiling—are still on hand. The peasant still is wearing his winter cape and hood in March, but at least he is outdoors, trimming his grapevines. April apparently was the peasant's favorite or most nostalgic month; a robust young man may be shown with an armful of flowers and ears of corn. May is a puzzle—perhaps the time for taxes—for it often is illustrated by a knight with a lance in his hand and a falcon on his wrist, while a peasant rests in the shade of a tree. Coming after the planting and before the long summer, May was a month of rest; but it seems curious that a peasant voluntarily would have a knight in what was supposed to be his own sculpture. In June the farmer could be carrying dried hay to the barn; in July he might harvest the corn; in August, swinging his flail, his shirt removed because of the heat, the peasant does his threshing. September is the month for treading barefoot in barrels of grapes for the wine maker. Sowing in October, the peasant has his winter cloak on again, and he leaves it on in November, when the winter's firewood is chopped

JEAN ROUBIER

and stacked. The December wedge is the most crowded of all: women bake cakes, the men slaughter pigs and cattle for the Christmas feast, and finally the revelers, wine glasses in hand, revel.

The trouble with the calendar was that it left the cathedral out of the peasant's life. His most festive times were spent there on the feast days; the important people whom he had seen he had seen there; he probably met his friends there. And some of his quietest times were spent there, too. He could sit on the floor, or on the long wooden benches placed in some cathedrals, for hours when he wanted to be alone. He could walk around and let the cathedral talk to him. The saints might give him a smile or a worried frown; the windows and tapestries might tell him things that he never had known about those very saints. At magical moments he could stand and watch the light shift and change colors as it poured down through the stained glass to glide along the marble statue in the niche. He was very much like that statue, although he probably did not realize it. Both he and it belonged to the cathedral, and both he and it were quite ready to break free.

In the calendar of the Cathedral of Amiens, the months (top row) are symbolized by signs of the zodiac, and the activities of the month are described beneath. Under Cancer, the crab (June), a peasant is reaping his hay; under Leo (July), he is harvesting; under the Virgin (a medieval symbol for August), he is threshing.

127

SAINTS AND DEMONS

Although the medieval artisan was obedient to strict rules for the carving of the main religious statuary of a cathedral, he gave free reign to his imagination when he designed the small decorative figures that adorned the exteriors. Shrieking and howling faces, half-comic and half-grotesque animals—all the most terrifying creatures from the mason's darkest nightmares rendered in stone. Providing a sharp contrast to the more prominent saintly figures, the creatures, called gargoyles, seemed to serve as a reminder to the worshipers of the sort of afterlife awaiting the unfaithful. And very often the demonic figures were used to serve as rainspouts as well. The monster at left sits high above Paris on the Cathedral of Notre Dame, relishing his prey. Directly above, the ape-faced monk from Lorraine Cathedral conceals a piece of support masonry. One of the most bloodcurdling gargoyles anywhere is the lion (right) on Laon Cathedral, crushing a child beneath him. The leering goblin at top right, in the Dijon Museum, and the winged and horned creature from Notre Dame at far right reminded viewers of the many guises used by the devil as he went about the evil business of tempting the innocent.

129

PLAIN AND FANCY

The decorative fixtures in many Gothic edifices were donated by merchants and aristocrats, and the lavishness of the church's appointments became a status symbol for the diocese. At far left on the opposite page is a painted wooden Virgin and child from thirteenth-century France—a touchingly tender but comparatively humble gift. More elaborate was the bejeweled cross at left, a sixth-century Visigothic relic given to the Cathedral of Oviedo in Spain. Below that, a ninth-century gold-mounted disc that became the paten of Saint Denis. At right, a gilt reliquary arm of Saint George. At Wells Cathedral in England there is a famous fourteenth-century clock, below, which showed the month and moon phase as well as the time and announced the hour with a quartet of jousting knights. Below, right, a gilt and bejeweled statue of Saint Foy, a product of many centuries: the head was made in the fifth century: the cloak, ninth; the crown and throne, tenth; and the crystal balls, fourteenth.

SACRED AND EARTHY

The great cathedrals of the Gothic Age were products of the labor of builders and of all the best artists and artisans of medieval Europe as well. Their contributions in wood, stone, ivory, and precious metals and gems provided the interior of each edifice with a character and atmosphere of its own. At far left on the opposite page is a wooden panel from a choir stall depicting the marriage of the Virgin. Such figures as the two at left, also carved of wood, decorated altars and screens: one is a victorious angel, and the other reminds the worshiper of the evils of drunkenness. Both figures are in Chester Cathedral in England. The medieval aristocracy designed elaborate tombs with great care and often without regard for cost. A typical tomb, below, at Christ Church at Oxford, is capped by a representation of the dead knight; his horse's head is his pillow. At right is one of the famous smiling angels of the Cathedral of Reims, and below that, on a column capital at the Cathedral of Wells: a man suffering from toothache.

133

VII

INTERNATIONAL GOTHIC

Early in the fifteenth century an Italian artist named Filippo Brunelleschi came upon a set of rules and principles for building drawn up by Vitruvius, a famous architect of ancient Rome. Brunelleschi, himself an architect as well as an accomplished sculptor, was fascinated by Vitruvius' writings, especially by their logical clarity, brevity, and simplicity. In order to measure the actual proportions of the buildings and to calculate the system of perspective used by the ancient builders, he journeyed to various Roman ruins. After studying their every detail, Brunelleschi set down his discoveries, which became the guidelines for a new generation of architects.

In 1421 the Medici family—who were emerging as the absolute rulers of the important little city-state of Florence —commissioned Brunelleschi to design a building. This structure would be the first of the new age called the Renaissance; and even before its completion in 1445, its impact would be reverberating throughout the Italian peninsula into a receptive southern France. Soon word of it would spread throughout all Europe. And word of it would forecast the end of the Gothic.

It was not, however, the Neoclassical style of the new architecture that doomed medieval architecture; nor was it the simplicity of Brunelleschi's building or the ready acceptance that it found. It was the idea of it, its reason for being. For the very first building of the Renaissance was not a great cathedral or even a humble church, nor was it a palace, a castle, or a country villa. It was a foundling hospital, a home for the orphaned and neglected peasant children of Florence.

For one thousand years people had been told that life

PHOTO, BULLOZ

This Byzantine-inspired Christ was made in thirteenth-century Germany for a church in France.

The Cathedral of Cologne, Germany (opposite), designed in 1248, was not completed until 1880, after the original designs had been rediscovered.

HELGA SCHMIDT-GLASSNER

135

was a test, that discomfort was but a slight sacrifice to ensure everlasting happiness, that pain, hunger, deprivation, and degradation were small prices for the reward to come. For ten centuries the banner of Christianity had flown over a society whose justification for its inhumanity and brutality was that life on earth mattered little, except as a test of faith and virtue. For three hundred years the peasantry had been taxed and driven to build magnificent cathedrals that the peasantry genuinely loved. Yet even the wonderful cathedrals had risen high above the peasant, like everything else, dwarfing him and making him feel small and insignificant. He had felt that he belonged to the cathedral, but he should have felt that he belonged to himself and that the cathedral belonged to him, too.

Brunelleschi's building contradicted the spirit of the Middle Ages. The foundling hospital said, in effect, that people—even the most humble people—were important here on earth, that the poor and helpless were entitled to a home and food and warmth and companionship in this life, not just in the next. It said that charity was as Christian an act as was worship. The first building of the Renaissance, then, was not a church, but it was in its way very much a Christian edifice.

If Florence's foundling hospital foretold the end of the Middle Ages, the fire of the cathedral crusade never was altogether extinguished. Indeed, from the time of Abbot Suger's church to the present day, Gothic sanctuaries have been built and rebuilt, and each nation of western Europe had its own imprint to make on the evolution of the style. Thus, even as the Renaissance flourished in Italy, the Gothic continued its Continental tour. But the crusading spirit gradually was disappearing.

Before retracing the northward and southward journeys of the master builders, we should look to the west, since only in the British Isles had the intense activity of the French cathedral crusade been matched. As we do, it is important to keep in mind that although interchanges of information and influences between France and England had been constant, their architecture had developed along significantly different lines. Because of these differences, many historians prefer to study medieval building in England as something unique and not really part of the Romanesque-to-Gothic process of the Continent.

A brief look at English cathedral building, however, will reveal how the character of a people and the geographical factors of a nation can reinterpret an artistic style.

When the Normans successfully invaded England in 1066, they brought with them a massive, weighty sort of building style that was very similar to the European Romanesque. In the twelfth century the transition from the Norman to the equivalent of the Gothic in England approximated the transition in France. Moreover, a number of French and English masons began traveling back and forth across the English Channel to work on cathedrals in both countries, and soldiers from both nations went crusading to the Holy Land and were impressed by Byzantine and Moslem architecture. In the middle 1100's the pointed arch characteristic of the Gothic appeared in both lands. A similar style of cathedral architecture seemed to be developing in both countries and probably would have emerged except for several organizational and geographical differences.

In France, as we have seen, the importance of the monasteries decreased while that of the cathedrals of the cities increased. The bishops of England, too, were becoming more powerful, but unlike their brethren in France, they were inclined to maintain a close association with their monasteries. Instead of building their grand cathedrals in the hearts of towns and cities, the English monks-turned-bishops preferred to build them alongside their abbeys, usually out in the country or suburbs. Thus, the cloisters and well-tended gardens, the walled porches and sidewalks associated with park-secluded monasteries became the settings for many of England's great cathedrals as well. Since the edifices were set in spacious parks rather than in

The Hospital of the Innocents, an orphanage, was built in Florence early in the fifteenth century. Its appearance foreshadowed the decline of the Gothic style.

crowded cities, they tended to look as tall as did the French cathedrals, although, on the whole, they were not as high. They were, however, longer, and while their naves were narrower, the churches characteristically sprawled over a larger area. This was so because a monastery or school often was built alongside the cathedral, connected to the main structure by a canopied porch or an elongated transept.

English builders also had a more dominant tradition to account for in their cathedrals. Like Continental history, that of England had been influenced by pre-Christian peoples who favored a decorative, very linear kind of art. In England, however, these people, the Anglo-Saxons, had developed artistic styles of much greater sophistication than those of the barbarian Franks, Germans, and other wandering tribes. When the Norman conquerors began building, they were required to employ local workmen, in addition

Unlike most French cathedrals, which usually were built within cities, English edifices more commonly were erected in the country, or at least in a spacious city park. Above is the Cathedral of Ely.

to the artisans whom they had brought from the Continent. Familiar with their own native decoration, which was geometrical and linear, the Anglo-Saxon workers introduced their traditional embellishment into the structures that they were building for the Normans. A linear quality thus characterized English medieval building from the start: the squarish towers over the crossings of most English cathedrals indicate that masons in charge decided to take advantage of these survivals of Anglo-Saxon tradition, so apparent on the pre-Norman fortress castles of the British countryside.

Britain is an island, and its strength or weakness long depended on its ability to defend the homeland from invasions from the sea and on its ability to conquer the seas separating it from the trade routes and riches of the Continent and the lands beyond. The Normans were the last to cross the Channel as conquerors; that they were successful testifies to their own ability as sailors. But the people whom they mastered also were experienced seamen. As conquerors and conquered merged to become one nation, they became the greatest sea power in history. That they were, interestingly, had an important effect on their architecture.

A people who rule the waves obviously know how to build splendid boats; the building of splendid boats requires superb use of timber and knowledge of carpentry. They must know how to choose the best timber for a special job, to curve it to the precise arch that will be strongest under stress, to join plank to plank perfectly to ensure watertight joints. It has been charged that the British were inferior to the French in their architectural stonework. After the start of the thirteenth century, however, stone vaulting gradually played a less conspicuous role in the building of English churches, and timber roofs became more elaborate and intricate. Woodwork was used throughout the churches where stone sculpture was used in French cathedrals.

In medieval England architecture changed from one style to another more gradually than did architecture on the Continent, and most of the great cathedrals there took long periods of time to build. Like many of them, Gloucester Cathedral contains elements of each of the four main stages of English medieval architectural development, called Norman, Early English, Decorated, and Perpendicular styles.

As the English styles underwent transitions removing them from the Middle Ages, the intensity of activity began

THE CATHEDRAL
OF GLOUCESTER

Although the medieval architecture of England and Continental Europe developed along approximately parallel lines, there were substantial differences between the resulting styles. Many of the variations reflected differences in the temperament of the people, their historical and artistic traditions, and the materials that were available and with which the workers were familiar. Built on the site of a pre-Norman Benedictine monastery and erected over a period of several centuries, the Cathedral of Gloucester contains examples of most of the major English styles. At the top of the opposite page is the exterior of a chapel in the Norman style, the eleventh-century equivalent of the early Romanesque in France. Some windows have been replaced but the stonework is the original Norman. The ambulatory of the south choir (right, above), first built c. 1090, is also in the massive Norman style. Above the great cloister in the photograph opposite, below, is the large-windowed transept in the Decorated style, the parallel to the French Gothic of Chartres and Notre Dame (Paris). Like the tower in that picture, the vaulted nave (right, below) is an example of the English Perpendicular style, the ornate, intricate counterpart to the northern French and German High Gothic.

to slacken in France. It is not difficult to determine why: there were just so many dioceses as the fourteenth century drew to a close, and one cathedral apiece was plenty.

Spain, meanwhile, was engaged in a struggle between Christian elements and the declining but still powerful descendants of the Moors, an Islamic people who had conquered the Iberian Peninsula in the eighth century. The complete expulsion of the Moors did not take place until 1492, but through the thirteenth, fourteenth, and fifteenth centuries, the Christians steadily increased their territory; the influence of the Holy Roman Empire grew stronger apace.

Part of this influence was architectural, and the Church leadership in Spain welcomed the glorious Gothic with open arms. The results were sometimes startling.

Seville Cathedral is the largest cathedral in Europe. (Only St. Peter's Basilica in Rome is, among Christian churches, larger; but St. Peter's, because it is not the seat of a bishop, is not properly a cathedral.) Built on the site of a Moorish mosque, Seville Cathedral is rectangular in shape and general layout; but even the added-on parts of the edifice, supposedly Gothic, reveal the lingering Moorish influence in the country. For every pointed arch there are several of the typically Islamic horseshoe arches; for every Gothic spire there are many vertical projections that look very much like the minarets of an Arabian mosque. The bell tower of the structure was in fact originally the famous twelfth-century minaret known as Giralda. Although the Moorish influence here is the extreme example in Spain, it did linger significantly in other less spectacular cathedrals.

The real slack caused by the French slowdown was picked up by the Germans and Austrians with their characteristic gusto. The masons of these countries studied the French cathedrals well and learned the organizational setup of the lodges. The churches that they produced were, on the whole, very similar to the cathedrals of the high Gothic in France; but efficient as ever, the northerners added refinements to the lodge system.

French masons (as well as those in England) always had maintained lodges that were independent of one another. There was a wonderfully co-operative attitude be-

Pictured at right is the spectacular Cathedral of Seville in Spain, erected during the fifteenth and sixteenth centuries over a Moorish mosque. The famous bell tower "Giralda" originally was a twelfth-century minaret.

tween lodges, and an impromptu interlodge meeting, called perhaps to help settle some difficulty, always would be well attended. But each lodge remained an entity in itself. Essentially, the French masons thus were admitting that the lodge belonged primarily to the cathedral—not to the bishop or chapter but to the building, which was the masons' principal concern.

The German and Austrian masons admired the cooperative spirit of the French lodges but not the haphazardness of their relations and the informality of their meetings. To profit most from the discoveries of their brothers, the northern masons grouped clusters of lodges into districts, districts into provinces, and so forth. There were regularly scheduled conferences and conventions at every organizational level; codes of conduct and standard building procedures were adopted. In this way the restrictions of one lodge became restrictions for all, everything in good order.

Although, on the whole, Italy was not especially fond of Gothic architecture, the churchmen in Milan decided in the fifteenth century to erect their new cathedral (right) in the style. Notable for its many spires, it is a rather German-looking structure, but that is because almost all the masons had to be imported from the north.

In some respects the uniformity of the northern lodges might have served to some advantage if their members had not loved rules so much. If a master at Cologne developed a very good system for raising scaffolding, the masons made a rule that this system had to be used everywhere. Lodges collected drawings religiously and insisted that members learn the proportions on them. There was so much to study, so much to memorize, so complicated a system to grasp that there was less and less opportunity for inventiveness. Villard d'Honnecourt, who had been able to master every aspect of building in the thirteenth century, would have gone mad trying to do so in the fifteenth century.

The efficiency of the later Gothic masons had not produced better Gothic buildings, but it had set the stage for the downfall of the Gothic. Should a simpler system come along, it would find plenty of younger masons waiting for it, ready to seize it.

And just such a system was on the way.

Worn down by recurring plague, but less concerned, because of their warm climate, about the effects of shelters, the Italians never had embraced the Gothic. The Byzantine tradition, with its emphasis on colorful and richly patterned decoration, suited them better. Their constant exposure to the ruins of ancient Rome made them feel closer to that highly developed civilization, and they tended to regard their Christian neighbors to the north as scarcely more than barbarians. As the Gothic achieved such obvious heights of technical expertise, the Italians responded by adapting some few Gothic forms to their own distinctive architecture. But more important, they took to digging through ruins.

As the Italians sought to uncover the Classical past—and thus stress their relationship to the peoples of the ancient Classical world—they stimulated a national interest in all things ancient. They excavated old libraries and civic buildings; they began rereading Classical poetry and reappraising Classical art. Their own poets began to imitate the style of the ancients; their own artists began to emulate the styles of antiquity. Thus did the Renaissance, or "rebirth" of Classicism, begin to gather momentum.

It was at this time that Brunelleschi discovered the writings of Vitruvius.

The French author Victor Hugo once observed that "The horizontal is the line of reason, the vertical the line of prayer." In the years, decades, and then centuries that followed the erection of the foundling hospital, the Christian world discovered that it had room for both horizontal and vertical, reason and prayer, the horizontal emphasis of the Renaissance style and the verticality of the Gothic. Although the cathedral crusade dwindled and the Gothic eventually lost its potency as a vital force in art, it never lost its presence. It has remained, to many people, the standard of monumentality by which all later styles must be measured. It has remained, surely, the "official" architecture of churches. Somewhere, always, a Gothic edifice is under construction or reconstruction and certainly scrutiny.

For one later bishop, the building of his cathedral recalled typical medieval problems. After sixty-five years the construction of his edifice came to a standstill for lack of funds. The bishop had offended some of the richest people in the diocese by his activities, and they had withdrawn their formerly generous support. That the cathedral was the world's largest in the Gothic style, that it was being constructed by traditional means that any medieval mason would recognize, made no difference: neither bishop nor donors would budge. Thus the plans were taken out and mulled over, and economic corners were cut and reductions were made as they had been made many times before. Reluctantly, the bishop said, he had decided that the twin towers of the west façade and the great spire of the crossing —those heaven-reaching elevations that are the pride of so many Gothic churches—would have to be eliminated from the plans.

It was the same old story with the same familiar plot, but the setting and the details had been updated. The sixty-five years of work had begun in 1902. The bishop was an Episcopalian in the archdiocese of New York City, and he had lost millions of dollars in pledges to his Cathedral of St. John the Divine because of his dedicated activities on behalf of the cause of human rights and equal justice for all men.

Then a summertime of strife demonstrated to the bishop that his cause was a long way from being achieved, and he announced suddenly that work on the cathedral would stop altogether. The money, he said, could be better spent helping the poor and deprived. The towerless, spireless cathedral overlooking the sprawling ghetto of New York's Harlem would remain unfinished until all men had come closer to living in accordance with the real spirit of Christianity. His unfinished cathedral, then, has become a symbol of a twentieth-century crusade.

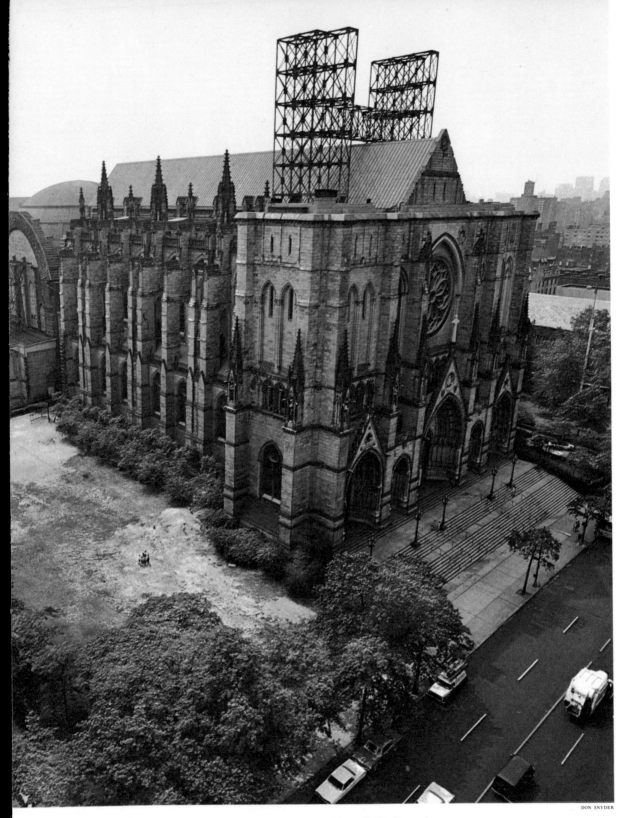

*Above, the Cathedral of Saint John the Divine in New York City. As
long as the squalor of Harlem behind it remains, its Episcopalian bishop
has declared, the huge twentieth-century edifice will remain unfinished.*

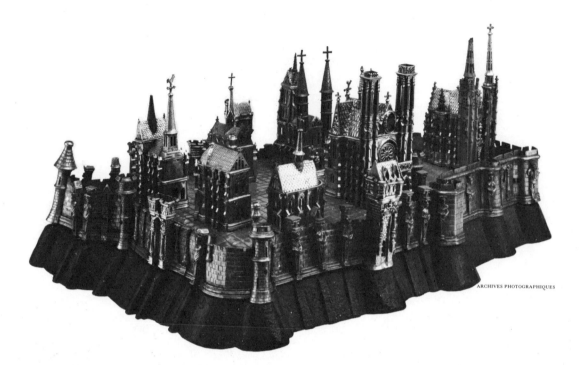

A celebration of the glory of the Gothic, this gilt reliquary, cast and chiseled of copper and silver, is a fanciful representation of the French city of Soissons. Although it was famous for its abundance of churches and monasteries, Soissons was not quite so single-minded as the model suggests. It also contained both humble and palatial homes, commercial buildings, factories, shops, and stables, as well as the many places of worship.

ACKNOWLEDGMENTS

The Editors are particularly grateful for the valuable assistance of Mrs. Claire de Forbin in Paris and Mrs. Mary Jenkins in London. In addition, they would like to thank the following:

Bibliothèque Municipale, Cambrai—Michel Bouvy
Bibliothèque Nationale, Paris—Marcel Thomas, Mme. Le Monnier
Bibliothèque Publique de Dijon—Pierre Gras
Pamela Hynds
Münster, Ulm—Dekan Dr. Seifert
Musée de l'Œuvre de la Cathédrale, Reims—Michel André
Österreichische Nationalbibliothek, Vienna—Hofrat Dr. Hans Pauer
Scala, Florence—Brigitte Baumbusch, Linda Berry

FURTHER REFERENCE

Readers who are interested in viewing examples of art and artifacts from medieval times will find exhibits at the Blackburn Museum and Art Gallery; the Fitzwilliam Museum, Cambridge; the National Museum of Ireland, Dublin; Dumfries Burgh Museum; the National Museum of Antiquities of Scotland, Edinburgh; Glasgow Museum and Art Gallery; Lincoln City and County Museum; the British Museum and the Victoria and Albert Museum, London; the Ashmolean Museum, Oxford; the Yorkshire Museum, York; and the Musée de Louvre, Paris.

For those who wish to read more about medieval times, the following books are recommended:

Adams, H. *Mont-Saint-Michel and Chartres*. New ed. Constable, 1950.

Anderson, M. D. *The Medieval Carver*. CUP, 1935.

Branner, R. *Gothic Architecture*. New Jersey: Prentice-Hall, 1962.

Carnage, D. *Cathedrals and How They Were Built*. CUP, 1948.

Fitchen, J. F. *The Construction of Gothic Cathedrals*. OUP, 1961.

Fletcher, B. *History of Architecture on the Comparative Method*. Athlone Press, 1961.

Gimpel, J. *The Cathedral Builders*. Translated by C. Barnes. Evergreen Books, 1961.

Harvey, J. H. *The Gothic World, 1100–1600*. Batsford, 1950.

Headlam, A. C. *Chartres*. Dent, 1902.

Male, E. *Religious Art in France in the 13th Century*. Translated by D. Nussey. Dent, 1913.

O'Reilly, E. B. *How France Built her Cathedrals*. Evanston: Harper & Row, 1921.

Prentice, S. *The Voices of the Cathedrals*. New York: William Morrow, 1938.

Simson, O. von. *The Gothic Cathedral*. Routledge, 1962.

Temko, A. *Notre Dame of Paris: the Biography of a Cathedral*. Secker & Warburg, 1956.

INDEX

Boldface indicates pages on which maps or illustrations appear

This miniature from a thirteenth-century French Bible depicts the good Persian King Cyrus watching the Hebrews, whom he had liberated, build their splendid Temple.

THE WALTERS ART GALLERY, BALTIMORE